FULL CIRCLE

Full Circle

Astrological Signs in Verse

Susan Ironfield

JANUS PUBLISHING COMPANY LTD
Cambridge, England

First published in Great Britain 2010
by Janus Publishing Company Ltd
The Studio
High Green
Great Shelford
Cambridge CB22 5EG

www.januspublishing.co.uk

British Library Cataloguing-in-Publication Data
A catalogue record for this book is available from the British Library

ISBN 978-1-85756-721-2

Cover Design: Janus Publishing

Printed and bound in the UK by PublishPoint
from KnowledgePoint Limited, Reading

Contents

Foreword	vii
Aries (21 March – 20 April)	1
Taurus (21 April – 20 May)	9
Gemini (21 May – 21 June)	17
Cancer (22 June – 22 July)	25
Leo (23 July – 23 August)	33
Virgo (24 August – 23 September)	39
Libra (24 September – 23 October)	47
Scorpio (24 October – 22 November)	57
Sagittarius (23 November – 22 December)	67
Capricorn (23 December – 20 January)	75
Aquarius (21 January – 18 February)	85
Pisces (19 February – 20 March)	95

Foreword

For many years, astrology has meant a great deal to me. Eventually, I felt the need to write the following cycle of poems, based on information from several works on psychological astrology, in English and German. This subject has made great strides in recent times, involving some new, still debatable factors which, at the time of writing, I was not able to take into account. With the exception of this, the content of the poems is as accurate as I could make it. Of course, any poetic developments of my own are unavoidably hard to distinguish from the common astrological stock.

A feature which involved more original research, and which I have been very happy to work on, is a celebration of various well-known names. These, apart from Shakespeare, are always mentioned under their sun sign or, in one or two cases, under other signs which are strong for them. Perhaps I should explain that an actual person's Sun sign – so-called star sign – is only a part, though nearly always the most dominant, of a complex whole. Furthermore, people manifest different levels of development; for example, they are turned more to the positive or negative side of any characteristic. Astrology, with its ancient continuing experience and expertise, is unique in giving a complete detailed picture of such interwoven subtleties. The archetypal signs described here are, however, not individuals, though they are personified and rendered as male or female – not always according to the usual allocation – for poetic purposes.

The readers I hope to reach are not only astrologers, but anyone not irrevocably averse to the subject and who cares about the study of human nature and culture. Finally, I want to warmly thank those who have helped me in this undertaking.

Human nature: text in twelve parts. Imagine
first the full round displayed, lore mandala,
rose-window, twelve-rayed across the dark,
vibrant but flat, to make the global legible.
The shaped separate bits of colour hold their right
share of light – graded, aligned, integrated
to images that mirror meaning in mind and matter,
in each signed sector. These are distinct but linked,
cyclic, elemental geometry of trines:
fire, earth, air, water, states of being
radiant-active, solid-bodily, gaseous-mental,
fluid-feeling. Behind the modal panels, planets
move and glow. Solar-drawn – but look up!
they are where they are, with sun and moon, around us.
The resonance of the macro-microcosmic field,
the archetypal governance, the guiding lights
of old gods are in every detail demonstrable.

Here the signs speak – are spoken to – as types.
But people are composite, although sun-centred.
Each life-chart weaves a world that time's transits
help to lead along a learning curve, to turn,
with luck and good management, negatives to positives –
not burned: warmed, not buried: firmed,
not dispersed: inspired, not drowned: resolved.

Aries (21 March – 20 April)

The ancient cycle starts here:
the first figure to find and love.
No need to search – he stands out
indubitable, straight, sheer,
then marches right up to me,
attractive, reassuringly real.
Already I know where I am with him.
Aries, man, you're good at beginnings,
so help me now to explore how
you bounded into the world, a boy,
shouting, 'I am! that's a fact.
Here I come, number one,
right out of my red dawn
head first – I'm on my way.
I want life, to live it out,
boldly go for it – but nobly.
Out of my centre juts a spear
of keen idealised desire
to be the primary ego-hero
in the forefront, superman!
I'm inflamed for the good fight
by new music begot of old
heavy metal of muscular drums
and blatant statement of brass trumpets,

but beating with purer, finer power.
With royal spiral pride of horns
I will ram the foul fortress,
hiding oppression and dishonour.'

A fresh, fortunate cardinal virtue
is potent in his here and now,
heading also for the future.
Humanity here manifests
a firm world, Mars-coloured,
sun-shot, with iron core
to every crimson corpuscle, feeding
arterial inner fire. Just feel –
his glowing electromagnetic charge!
This tight elastic energy bounces
back, reacts roundly to knocks,
eager, kinetic, abrupt, bright.
Impetus and hot impulse
are primal in this vibrant primate.
Dynamic adrenalin must demand
decisive quick release of urges
in action. And extreme exertion
of work frees from pressure of what
must be achieved before the frequent
cooled, emptied-out withdrawal …
but soon refuelled, the self-renewal.

Oh, you game player, you.
Suddenly sighting the ball, aggressive,
you surge up and hard-head it
(with unreliable aim?), while
your emblematic brows curve

up like spring cotyledons.
Leaping, you overlook what lies
in front of your feet and risk stumbling –
but go! Go in and win –
prove your reality in contest
or conquest of the outer world,
but not as warmonger – no!
though often ferrous, febrile, feral.
The first ego-goal is life,
carefree lust of basic being
and going your own wilful way.

You have a strong brain and steely
eye of surgical penetration,
but jump to head-on conclusions.
Think how Descartes, of the startling eyebrows,
takes his time to think that he is
because he thinks – no doubt of that.
In practical matters you're persistent:
'No problem. I can do it
without your advice' – and set about it.
Impatient of lateral complications
but curious about cause and effect,
focused, sparked by intuition,
you find out your own solutions,
well able to mend what's broken
if you will – will finds a way.

Feelings are not much examined:
onset of anger or love, a sudden
conflagration, illuminating
seductive and transfigured images.

But high humanising ideals
elevate passion and expression.
A great worship is in you, intense,
instinctive sense, pristine, young,
of something simple, direct, splendid,
what we used to call sublime.
Mature unfolding of you will hold
sadness too of human language,
but never forgetting the vision, the gleam
the child self of Wordsworth felt.

In company – who do you think you are?
You seem to be quite sure of it,
yet all that demonstrative and cheerful
predominance is not stable:
you drop by without warning,
wanting to assume you're wanted.
Oh, you're ginger, mustard! gestures
vehement and insistent, opinions
antagonistic in argument,
stimulated by competition.
Tactless, inclined to overrule,
you break bounds but then regret it.
If ever dampened by defeat,
with touching Chaplinesque charm
you perk up and never give up.

Although your own lights may blind you
to others' character, views and values,
your mind hacks and burns hypocrisy,
believing in its own sincerity.
Injuries are soon freely

forgiven, forgotten – trust in goodness
blossoms up, however stamped on.
Open, lovable verve and positive
optimism win through.
What a big, generous soul –
you must go your own road,
but let others go theirs.

Eros is surely the son of Mars.
Psyche felt those fierce wings
above her and love-hunger, hard,
deep as ruby, struck her through.
She didn't, and then did, know him
and had to leave the palatial glory
she thought could be her rosy home.
Eros flies around like fever,
a quick quiver of hot darts.
Sight of the quarry sets a sharp
flame that soon fizzles out.
But first, the stirred, dashing dream
rejuvenates, like April sap
entering a green and flowering time.
You rise at the challenge of a conquest.
Is it a privilege of your nature
to take? yet, forbidden fruit
or honour, which comes first?
True to self above all,
somehow you seem justified
by an inner innocence
and fate gives you what you want.
You dominate then, but fear dependence,
until, 'I don't need you!' you blurt

with shocking candour, and stalk away.
'Why do they whine when it's over?
You can't expect a joy to last.'
Yet your pride was knifed, perhaps.
But in the end you can be a durable
jewel for the right partner,
true all through in trust and loyalty.
You bring your love home at last,
fight to keep her, fight her battles –
so long as she gives you your head,
and support: for purposes and visions
and ideas that warm the blood
for new beginnings to baulk boredom.

Play or work: first it's pure
physics, energy in motion.
Add: courage, clear intention,
wilful exercise of strength,
commitment without compromise.
Such a furnace may forge art.
Instances: Van Gogh's incisive
swirls and wild vibrations, Goya's
vivid expressionism, vital,
direct, edgy and relentless,
forcefully denouncing violence.
And Bach – rebellious with bosses,
he kept on his unswerving track.
Organ king, he helped build them
and wielded, welded fit and function
of endless works, ingenious engines,
invention inextinguishable
of ever-running, pulsing life –

with lovely fugal wheels in wheels –
yet organic, moved and moving
with human and divine feeling.
Haydn fathered the classical order
of symphonies like conscious beings,
growing form both spontaneous
and constructed (Surprise, Clock!).
Creation became his Oratorio
and each quartet's a microcosm
of speaking emotion or natural humour.
What a spring there is in him,
deeper than any storm and stress
of carefree healing happiness.

Now, could you as composer
re-conceive art for us?
mastering today's technology
with an intellectual rigour,
breaking, renewing old forms,
restoring early savage eloquence
and joyful, natural rhythmic dance,
to bring back colour to our faces –
and hymns for everybody's ears –
though love of God requires the best.
Reflector of the collective soul,
you're tough enough to grapple grimness
into a light of positive values.

Whatever your field of enterprise,
you like to enthuse young people.
A teacher's aim is to give and guide,
and, like a doctor of souls and bodies,

incite corpuscles against infection,
promoting germinating wholeness.
A beacon of any organisation,
you help, encourage individuals
in group dynamics and pioneer projects,
rousing their imagination,
inspiring them in their attempt
to regenerate social culture.
'Never give up hope,' you say.

That 'I am' is not in doubt.
Now you ask, 'What am I, then?'
and undertake your self-tuition,
to learn from experience and advice,
to study a thing before you try it
(is it impatience or pride drives you?)
to think: what is my right goal?
and take time for careful plans
and carry work to a conclusion.
To closely question your convictions,
consider consequences of acts
and see others' points of view.
To be fearless but not scornful,
your confidence cleansed of arrogance.
To invest virility in virtue.

Carbon, basis of life, survives
fire. Its crowning crystal form,
transparent, strong and authentic,
is diamond, displaying colours of energy,
like your true and best self.

Taurus (21 April – 20 May)

That was a wild encounter. We can now
rest a while by the earthly side of Venus.
Here, 'Taurus' means as much the female:
May woman – I'll try in relaxed, unmodern
lines to bear out, embody your being.

The lie of old land in you is profound
and holds for us a real corporeal peace,
and bland nature-bound voluptuousness
the solemn goddess warns us not to scorn.
Now let there be time to contemplate
a 'home-thought', common but evocative:
a meadow deeply married to moon waters
drowses. A cow dawdles with the herd,
now lowing with lugubrious vibrancy,
now bowed down, cropping slowly
the sweet herbs and flowers, with meek mouth.
She lies down to doze all afternoon,
then stands on brown mud, sturdy, steady,
with broad back and brow, and gentle look
fixed brooding on the boundary hedge
of opulent hawthorn, her nostrils rounded out
to odorous evening. But, the poor soul
is easy to abuse for mass nutrition,

for bulk of solid meat and mechanised
lactation. So it is an obsolete idyll,
dubious, partly bogus, yet its message
feeds the heart's blood like mother's milk.

So how is it with you, Taurus person?
Your dense self-identity of substance
consolidates land that Aries' impetus won.
Your clay of life is dug, pugged and pressed
to an anthropomorphic corpulent pot, potent
cavity to conceive your future self.
Durable power binds being, extends
its value into all kinds of having –
wanting first to hold what's familiar,
fond of the body, abode, bed and board.
The Freudian principle, in this physical world,
is pain avoidance, then the close indulgence
of senses, for pleasure, prior to cognition:
the luxury of smooth cream in the throat,
comforting cloth of quality, warm wood,
beads of glossy wood-born amber, all
tactile talismans of settled security.
They're hoarded in a large, solid house
clothed in roses – perhaps your place of birth,
your long home, your own quiet holding,
stately real estate of mid-county,
folded in that rich, imagined farmland.
Here, community festivals are continued,
earthbound dance, song and spread food,
traditional garb – the conserving way of life
that nourishes the full bloom of enjoyment.

Taurus (21 April – 20 May)

Your landscape is like one Gainsborough remembered,
his first love he made half-Arcadian,
on fat soil the massy leafage of Suffolk,
with generously rendered rustics and gentry.

But bloated possession can turn to obsession.
Your forebear Buddha came, a young prince,
to break through the high, elaborate bulwark
guarding the haves from the have-nots – and taught
to let go the fearful grasp of having
that constipates and darkens with excess
and with its converse shadow, deprivation.
So what kind of goods are truly good?

My own conceptual words seem rather weak
for boring down to the emerald lode of your life:
clogged under a dull dislike of abstract,
symbolic speculation, sleeps a gleam
of longing for a lightening of spirit.
I delve after communion with the mind
below the dumb stare – or else the blustering –
that hint at what you hardly know yourself.
You handle the stuff of what feels normal,
the real what, before the how or why,
but even unbending dogma may protect
from intuition deeper than you think.
Duly doled knowledge will be soberly
browsed, absorbed and well ruminated –
even relished – and stored in strong memory.
Learning is more by doing, slow and sure.

Understanding is gleaned from experience
and common sense; its pragmatic purpose is
to materialise, corroborate and confirm
existence: as oaks that draw up the bole
sustenance for great greening boughs.

Half buried in the body of the instincts,
how stable or controlled is your emotion,
I wonder, and how passive under placid
stillness, where raw hurt endures, until
it even provokes to trampling bellowing rage,
or skin becomes thickened against the prod,
the soul blunted. And then, perhaps, the sympathies
are safely invested in things to fill out
the hollow core, the doleful inner depletion.

There is a soft intensity and an earnest
sentimental memory of the pastoral
past age of the grounded agrarian group,
and frowning mistrust of later urbanely rational
restless culture, the scattered world beyond.
But out of this regression, planted deep
down in the coddling bed of mother earth,
more bulb than clod, you grow in round,
firm affection, to foster the near and dear.
Flesh and blood and lover are fed, defended,
given hugs and made to wrap up well –
for you are Freya's child, loving and giving.
Responsive yourself to such caring, you wish
it could be truly mutual: longing for more,
touchy, you may retire in sulky silence.
But by and large, you live with the status quo,

uncritical, easing into compromise
and bravely able to bear others' burdens.
The impulse of Aries is through love to life,
your own yearning is for love itself,
felt in physical presence and sexual pleasure.
You could be one of his admired princesses,
murmuring 'come and see me in my castle'
(Mars and Venus, a problematic pair ...).
Now I'm bombarded with typical obdurate images:
May queen, wreathed like a ritual heifer,
daughter of Aphrodite and bovine Hathor –
or clichés of hearts and flowers in some boudoir –
or alluring pictures made by men for men:
the female reclined – coy, languid curves
of banal doll – or revered idol of beauty?
(How brutal, if the bed's a site of butchery,
as gorgeously displayed by Delacroix:
Sardanapalus has his harem slaughtered.)
But then, by the cows' meadow, that lovely symbol,
an indolent dove full-breasted among blossom
redolent of Beltane, soothes the unmoving
air with velvet voice, an incantation
of harmonious wooing, and constancy to follow.
This confident and composed womanhood
is grave, magnetic – a passive will to bonding
of bodies and by that, bonding of selves
conducts the life current like coiled copper.
The force of passion comes on gradually
and unless blind, destructive, holds out
for marriage at last, the old to have and to hold.
Then, doubtfully, you're drawn towards the spirit
your man conveys, to fire or fan your dampness,

but find it hard to trust what is intangible.
His light freedom threatens to dislodge you,
makes you cling and demand equal loyalty.
At least you try to blot out jealous thoughts,
the inevitable corrosive devastation.
A good domestic partner keeps a balance:
not to dominate with moody controls,
not to be bogged in obedience like a boulder,
to be sensitive and forgiving – a fulfilled
archetypal lover, wife, mother:
so a goddess becomes a grown human.

Impressive immobility packs power,
holding back until sure of its purpose:
there is a large capacity for toil,
practical, regular, disciplined, determined:
the business may be movables, immovables,
land, property, money or art treasures.
You could make novels out of all that,
along with other passions, like Balzac –
framed like an ox and worked like one.
The field he ploughed: material and emotional
daily lives, greedy for wealth and love.

For you, a refining love is the world of music,
Natural, moving, intimate body of sound
and grounded coherent structure, emulating
palpable form of fibres growing together,
root and branch and new singing leaves.
As Brahms was rooted: in the fertile domain
of classicism, watered by folk melody.
His heavy symphonic soul then struggled on,

trudging lonely acres and long country,
a winding road, following hope of home.
He moves through and over his bleak hunger
and stamps it into big affirmation
of hearty timbre and warm, sensuous texture.
All-pervasive love is hardly bitter,
but ponders a buried resonance, a mystery.
Think of all the songs, the rhapsodic alto,
piano works like tender, hefty angels,
vast concertos: cello with violin,
a dream of double devotion, too remote.
So join the choral prayer for death and rest
after patient waiting for growing seeds
and future gathering into maternal comfort,
the home from home of lovely holy dwellings.

Even art can seduce as pseudo-wealth
or perverting of the link into a levelling
of sacred and profane love. But if
you're meant to make an art for our time
in the light of old revised, collective values,
authenticated by your own life,
then hold up your Venus mirror to nature's
dreadful, wonderful harmonic face
and produce the image as a power for good,
a beauty that transcends form and matter.
And make of yourself a work of art – learning
courage to stand up on your own basis
of self-value, growing up from the pull
of race, custom, opinion – opening out
to change, and looser, wider possibilities –
and budding out your imponderable birthright.

Gemini (21 May – 21 June)

No sooner do I think I need a breath of air
than my young, slender friend wafts in, smiling,
and lights up the room with scattered remarks and glances:
'Hi! I was out and about and – oh, look at that!'
He flits about, fingering things, poking his pointy
nose into my books. And now his mind perches
back on his twiggy body, that tensile nerve-tree
(tree that travels – he soon tore up those Taurean roots).
His quick words and gestures are eager to convey
his latest enthusiasm, all-arts cabaret
for his theatre: 'a filigree phantasmagoria,
satirical text, masked mime, dance, decor ...
I thought of Stravinsky's ballets and I might adapt
something from Petrushka – the lure of the fair, the puppet
strung up, manipulated, or a human soul?
Can you see me in his Harlequin garb (with guitar,
like Arlecchino, to exploit my own dexterity)?
I won't miss a trick!' No, you tricksy Ariel,
your versatile talent will manage the whole airy magic.
I try to keep track of the coolly sun-reflecting,
restless Mercury man, just now in transit
around his skidding orbit towards the next appointment:
'Hold on – that plays a part in my project,
to trap your dance in shape-shifting, wrong-footing
hemiola hexameters, keeping me on my toes.

And if your mobile mind will wait long enough
for me to focus the dazzle, I'll try to trace the fine
facets, Gemini gem, twinkling over your shadow.'

'What flattering attention – but I think you intend
to plot and net the zigzag flight of your poor fly,
pinning me down, dissecting wings and brittle skin
and delicate inner systems, the two-sided symmetry.
You'll talk me through myself, investigate my genes,
as if I were some philological drosophila!
You think you're clever, don't you? Do you really suppose
the truth of me would show through my surface charm?
To see myself is *my* task and even my text.
After all, I'm also a literary type.
But all right – this is a new conversational
game – so watch out, the ball's in your court.'

'More like several balls to keep in the air at once.'
Facts, that is, about his paramount intellect, fed
largely on facts through education and enquiry.
Sharp senses supply a skimming awareness that scans,
pecks and picks over all possible data.
Alert, objective, logical, he checks, questions, analyses,
(much as I do now, reflecting him). He also
oscillates between poles – pro and contra,
positive–negative, real–ideal – such diverse
dualities or multiplicities – an overview?
'You sling round mind and world acrobatic Puck's
girdle, or more, a mesh of online neurons, your
wide web of curious knots or nodes, to link you
up – or snag you?' 'Snag my winged feet – or maybe
the floating tissues of all my information theories

will shred in my breezy wake? But words, sweet cords,
connect me to experience, even if at a distance:
my cognitive communicative net, my way
to detect, to know, to tell, as if we cast a spell
of nomenclature on nature – a *Systema Naturae* –
did you know Linnaeus was Gemini? his generic
binary Latin labels for fauna, flora and minerals
banned the multilingual babble. Marvellous names:
ephemeroptera, atricapilla – campanula
(oh! my "cap and bells" – am I the Fool or the Genius?)
though classification is to some extent factitious
and cuts the continuity of endless variation.
One should learn to distinguish distinction from division!'

'I'm glad you have the wit to limit the role of Adam,
peering intently over your own mind's shoulder.
As if your secret task is to monitor your being,
dividing and then trying to piece yourself together
inside the input of whirring signals – but are you still
afraid to touch that integrity through the frail layer
of feeling, with its tight integument, baffle of terms?
As if you can't bear sighing out to a sunset
without retreating into a rational account.
Is this one clue to your confusing duality?
Some polarise differently their pendulum propensities,
like Elgar, and like Schumann (in soft Eusebius
and fervent Florestan: how noble they are ...)
Oh, the caprice of these composers, the fantasy, the sensitivity,
the *Wand of Youth*, the *Album for Youth*, and *Carnaval* ...
You split and blend, making me blink and see double,
at first bright, effervescent, then moody, morose,
with extreme exclamations, "Wonderful! Disgusting!"'

'Ow! now you're probing and pulling me apart
and you say I'm critical. Allow me my free being,
my light touch and go. Don't stifle my genie
in that specimen jar of yours or force my fresh growth.
As for feeling, do you think I'm a cold elf,
who fears, even resents love? Hmm ... maybe.
Well, why not put me to the test, at least
for amusement, for a fling? Aren't you anyway
seducing me? with this abrasive stroking stimulus,
this bandying of talk, half-bantering barter
of commendation and carping – the backhand compliments
of our verbal tennis. Admit, I do interest you!'

'Now now, you're a sly, sardonic enchanter, you think
you want to try to tempt, but what does your heart say?
Wild card, joker, what then is your suit?
However much I admire you, I think you'd lead me a dance,
fool me with your fickle twirl, pivoted swivel
in the wind of change. Tell me, whether vain
to serve your turn, weathervane? and by the way,
how about your "orientation" anyway?'
'You mean my right-hand, left-hand whirl with boy or girl.
Oh well. Then, I'll stay duty-free
and wait and sigh in secret, until my other half
will show me to myself without so many words.
You and I are more like fraternal friends,
a clear place for open and cheerful conversation.
And, being a sort of townie, just up my streets
is quite an assortment of contacts, to feed my curiosity,
to talk at and round, networking various needs.

I do admit, all your applause fans my wit –
as Puck pleads, "Give me your hands if we be friends,"
and that goes for acquaintances or even mere strangers.'

'You bounce back your image from all eyes and ears.
Aren't you afraid the "mirror of malicious eyes"
will damage your Yeatsian dialogue of self and soul –
if not malicious, then, like me, often muddled,
whenever you're mocking, irreverent, teasing or evasive,
or testily polemical, or trivialise things or yourself.
I hope my mirror doesn't craze you into fragments ...
for mostly you are likeable and liking, a fair,
altruistic, easy-going go-between,
turning to each in turn, balancer and juggler
of interests, forger of links or undoer of tangles.
An idea: you could make it your vocation,
doing us all a good turn, to clear a path
among the partly cancerous cobweb of cybernetics!'
'Yes, I could be a mediator, an interpreter,
unravelling the plot of chats, blogs and dot-coms,
and calling to reason the media and technology,
all the actual ultra-modern world-stage
sets – funfairs and unfair trade fairs, whatever –
I could turn my hand to that – on the other hand ...'

'I know: you love to handle books and magazines,
and would enjoy the teamwork of a publishing firm,
or selling, or lending. Or you could be in journalism,
your finger on the pulse of these neurotic times,
debunking humbug or winding back political spin,

showing that ends do not justify the means
and otherwise eloquent in promoting right ideas.'
'You mean, your ideas. So you're not afraid
I'd perpetuate sleaze or atrocious punning headlines?
Actually, I once had an idea for a journal –
'Artweave', a colloquium for various colleagues,
even dead ones, as in Schumann's Band of David,
to preserve the intrinsic values and the honour of art.
But oh – haven't you read my heart's real wish:
I'm young yet, but hope in time to turn my knowledge
to wisdom and make of elusive ideals a major work.
It's a question of belief that always hinders me:
my intellect suspects that over-scepticism
turns into naivety, that reason becomes sterile,
our grid lacks gravitational curves to centres of truth.'

'It's that old dilemma of essence and existence.
Sartre, for example, judged existence meaningless,
without real roots and even rather nauseous:
but man creates his own non-transcendent essence
on roads to freedom of choice of an authentic act.
There's no world soul, he thought, it's up to us.'

'Yeats, also, was rather squeamish about the contingent,
complexity and corruption. I know how he felt –
I hate muck and mess. And he faced up to worse.
He cared for lasting aristocracies of art.
For him, mystical essence was surely pre-existent
in unity of body and soul, dancer and dance.'

Gemini (21 May – 21 June)

'Your dancing spirit of reason also has wings,
to raise your flat spin into a widening "gyre".
Is Yeats one of your soul's dancing and singing masters?
He also adored geometry, "divine because empty and measured",
that ancient, sacred lore divulged to us by Dürer.'

'Yes. Yeats wrote how pure dynamic maths
informs the mind and how its figures express desire
for freedom and fulfilment of soul, in the relation
of two gyres or spirals, from above and from below
(reminding me of introvert and extrovert twins,
who must link and so learn one another)
and this is the energy of the human aura.
Aha! that gives a matrix for the mapping of my scheme,
a stage-work with moving geometry and verse,
but serious this time, interpreting lofty symbols,
daring at last to move into the middle of feeling,
a final delineation and fledging of my spirit.'

Now I say 'wonderful!' and – have a good flight!

Cancer (22 June – 22 July)

Imagine the quiet rhythm of evening waves
cooling a July beach. Most of the families
have gone, leaving shapes of their absence, but still
the woman lingers on the sand, drawn,
tide-like, by the moon her meek face
mirrors. Her slack, flowered frock hides
a waxing foetus in his rounded sea,
the pulsing flood his cradle song. Her first
child holds her hand, herself enfolded
with mother in enchantment – chilled by fear.
Will this daughter, carrying her own
guiding moon, ever walk free
without that hand to save her in her dreams?

The mother herself is childlike, bland, mild,
her face a cup trembling to the rim
with feeling: sadness, regret, joy, hope,
delighted amusement bubbling in a laugh
and mere amazement at the sublunar world.
This avatar of more than one goddess
appeals, impresses with deep impersonal power,
which moves around the inwardness of cycles,
of moods, of seasons, of own bodily changes,
ovulation, birth, growth and death.

I want to see, know and love this being
signed in counter-rotating currents, and try
to sense the flow of inert, ambiguous water.
It seems limpid, simple, but its behaviour
is not. Seas are obscure and also veins
of groundwater – I need to be a dowser
or to lean on the swell of rising falling emotion.
To learn her also means to honour the moon,
white elusive eye, alarming and loving,
whose gravity is greater than the sun's
over the close earth. All fluids obey
the pervasive pull – secret lymph-like pools
of life like fecund matriarchal cauldrons,
stirred or still vessels lending visions.
Keeping my own head above water,
I peer down here for a dubious view:
under reflections, refractions of the primordial
mere, magic solvent for potent plasma –
a vast, amorphous *Amoeba proteus!*

Her evolution esteems her own insides,
like wet bundles to bear, be borne with – breasts,
stomach to digest, womb to gestate,
kidneys cared-for, careworn water babies
and heart often heavy with its humours.
Waterlogged and overwhelmed, she strives
to maintain the thin containment, skin or shell,
warding off turbulence outside –
or inside, often leaking out in tears.
She shrinks and draws back from hurt and threat,
needing and fearing to feel and be felt:

the crabby armour between her and the world
is so fragile, however reinforced
against all the sucking and the rending.

Family love is first, linked to dread
of loss of people and things – and of the unknown:
a cloudy atmosphere of insecurity.
She's rocked, shaken by melodramatic surges
of ecstasy and despair, horror, pity,
melancholy and bright enthusiasm.
But at the source is pure self-healing.
Her faithful wisdom is a moonlit mystery,
part of the great mass-unconscious, lulled
in dim breathing of the soul of things
and subtly responsive to the weather of fate.
She wonders, self-communing, wound like wool
around the navel of her formative memory,
her own, her people's – yet history may hinder
any move towards personal freedom.

Passive to nature's rhythm, she holds back
from clock-time – our demands, decisions decant
her balance – we must wait until she's ready.
Her present is soaked in observations, printing
her mind like molecular memory of water.
But often the straight clear rays of perception
are deflected to a misty inverse mirage
of pointless or invalid information,
sentimental prejudice, projection,
exaggeration and self-defensive inventions.

This amiable being should not be blamed,
if moisture blears the too affective sight
and rusts to a blunt blade the intellect
anyway more apt to dissect than discern
our symbiotic organic processes.
And, among all naive, swollen images,
superstitions, fantasies, illusions
and monsters only a mother can remove,
her longing for true conception is also granted:
imagination that gives life to reality,
making of her a grail of the good dream.

The task of finding others is compounded
with finding the cardinal core of self – authentic
but swamped by a shy sense of being inadequate
in a smart world. Without rational dialogue,
real intuition and compassion
can be contorted by the ego, assuming
that others share one's own ideas and wishes.
She flows into whatever container she thinks
you see her in and desires so to be held,
but the measure is short or runs over. Conversely,
she makes you the chalice for her life – but you
won't be lived in by that tilting weight!
If only she could meet a connecting vessel,
discover a deep link, an even level.
But so, misreading others and being misread,
she's first enraptured then slighted, plaintive, sullen.

Such ambivalence of emotional pressure
bewilders: the wary hiding away or the trustful
clamping onto strangers as familiars,

then abruptly dropping you and backing off.
She withdraws her help, or else heaps it on,
like presents you're embarrassed not to want.
Her sacrifice may be to win love
or her own pleas for help a kind of plucking
on your half-guilty motivation to care.
She wears down resistance in this circle
of wish-fulfilment, giving and receiving.
Fear of rejection tends towards tyranny –
or would she fatten her man, to swallow him whole?
Possessive nurture could castrate his will,
a mother's boy. She drifts towards the image
of father or son, to make her dependent or dominant,
docile or doctrinaire – he must be obeyed,
or trained. Where's the balance of equals? unless
a real empathy can stabilise.
Here is so much needy love to give
and yearning eyes beg for firm, intimate
reassurance – then she's devoted.
She hardly dared to hope for midsummer marriage,
but ancient Anima, like Beauty secluded
in timeless sleep, draws him who is able
to reach her sanctum by his own wisdom,
shielding his eyes from thorny, clinging briars.

Moon is, differently from Venus, domestic.
The home opens its arms, harbouring the animate
and, with animistic concern, the inanimate:
clutter to clad this nostalgic caddis worm
or odds and ends of crafts, mementos, emblems,
balmy with many old and new notions.
Bowls, jugs and jars are receptive round her

and hold – the family's body and soul together,
though too much pudding love softens up
and stunts – breast milk must give way to bread
and not to guzzling or to helpless boozing –
filling overfull is no fulfilment.
But mothering as secure, steady benevolence
brings embedded embryos to term,
then like a white wadded light cover
over the small creatures, fosters them,
without stifling nature by too much nurture.
The place of work is also a caring home,
for children or animals, or an organisation
for funding good causes. Her charity longs
to feed the world's hunger – a power for good
or a good that stays so by refusing power?
That, Iris Murdoch understood.
It seems to me she understood everything
about the psyche, sordid and sublime,
emotions, thoughts, relationships and destinies,
and *Metaphysics as a Guide to Morals.*

So huge hunger and thirst of the spirit
may compel to a welling of creation
in the fullness of time. The mind's depths
lodge the settled leaves of old cultures
and all immersed remembrance gleaming up
as time lost and found, as it was for Proust.
Under the melting light of a tearful, mellow
transcendence, her fecundity rounds out
the flesh of all her somnolent contemplation
and passive mulling over of order and form.

Awhile she's discontented, that lack of clarity
and dilatory brooding delay completion:
until her tenacity hauls out of the loose
impressions and liquid colours the speaking figures.
So whimsical Chagall drew from his visions
a poetic pageant of home, land and heart.
And Rembrandt, with his real reflective look
and soul's intelligence, made emotion studies.
His portraits gaze through layered glaze – his own
face is everyone's, everyone's face is his.
In stills that catch the constancy of change
are painful drama, doubt, everyday humour,
tragic resignation and moral stamina,
great strength out of great weakness.
More immensely from the diffuse flow
of sound grew the plangent Mahlerian song
of earth and humanity, doomed or enduring,
led also by the eternal feminine hand,
through horror and banality and grandeur.

Once a moon person moves to leave
home and mother, moves from emotion to form
and action – she prints her replete paragraphs
on palimpsests of the past. Her loving lessons:
to bear bravely the soul's fluctuations
and not be overset, and feel with others
in their difference, and help them to bear.
She may make it the stuff of world art
or pour her life into simple lyrics,
embracing the universal in the personal:

'Here, where I am, it seems calm,
by this mere, under the moving moon,
mimicked by puffed globes of shy mushrooms
and leaning umbels' lace. In their shade,
a damp snail tries his dubious horns.
How can you think that, just because I hide,
my slow, cringing mollusc heart is hard?

'The rapt scene is a pane breathed over
with silver and behind it is my longing:
your landscape, which the moon links to mine.
Calm around – but now the water shivers,
lifting the dim, folded lily-pad –
a foetal frog slips in fear from the lip.
Waves inside me spread further, further:
I dream of safe passage to your far
coast, then wish you here in my home-haven,
not all at sea but like a boat cradled
on inland water, a close, complete world.
Come to where I am: my lunar gravity –
strong or weak? – is pulling on your love.
But do believe I'm humble, I will drop
my clinging hands, my wet eyes and wait
through phase after phase of the moon.'

Leo (23 July – 23 August)

Another blaze! hot Aries hurtled, but Leo holds
his place, lets his radiance range the wide, admiring world
and holds rule, a royal solar orb of self-gold,
over the high summer and the timeless now of noon.
So the sun comes to its own sign and eponymous image
emerging in the bush, where he struts in tawny light,
the lion: will he be pleased by my portrayal of him here
(if not obscured by all my lanky undergrowth of lines)
or angry, lashing his tail? Just look at him, totally beautiful,
romping with big, alarming, playful paws or else roaring
ready to act! or lying, rolling long, leisurely hours,
lifting now and again his pompous head and sagacious eyes.
So he holds court, imposing, splendid, with his resonant
confidence and lusty, vibrant laughter from the heart.

Born firm and manifest out of moon woman's diffusion,
rounded, undoubted ego one and whole, this aware hero
comes a conscious culmination of all foregoing elements,
renewed here in flaring energy and relaxed foresight,
working towards unfolding self's full, ultimate harmony.

Meanwhile, enjoyment's growth potential can run rank
into a gambling waste and greed, a widespread wild gambol
of hedonistic luxury – but how he does exult
in regal distribution of his rich, animate substance.
What a strong, magnificent being, bright with will to power,
revealed in grand, exuberant wielding of warm heart's worth,
wisely moderating imperial Napoleon's megalomania!
He feels his value as free liver and fond, happy giver
of life – his smiling inner sun means to make our day,
like radial flowers that image him, arrayed round his zenith.
His soul he knows his own, he is his own natural law
and wants to be ours, too, but that is largely because he loves us.
Tolerance towards his children softens his despotism!

Shall we, dim, damp creatures, lift up our faces,
to take his charismatic glory as a fact of life,
burning through our cloudy view of the world – or of him?
By divine right, this central light disposes us as planets.
He can be a bombastic, flamboyant beast, but he is courteous,
conscious of caste but also of obligations of nobility,
and he welcomes us to the glamour and lustre of his golden house.
Paternal protection and aid like the rayed hands of Ra
reach down to animals, friends, the family he founds,
the clan, the nation. Moon people hanker back for these –
he will get them organised and bring them into the present,
draw them into his drama, where he's protagonist and producer.

He plays out his own persona, to do himself justice,
knowing it seems conceit, but anything less is near deceit.
Yet fearing flattery, he asks, 'Am I really genuine?'
His globe of self is whole, but quivers around inner conflicts:
self and role, ideal and real, expression and authenticity.

And sometimes people shun a light that shows up stains:
then his flame falters as if the blame is partly his.
Damage to his proud image makes him look so droopy
that many admirers are only too glad to reassure
and caress the big cat, who gives so much to prove himself
and resents, but soon forgives, any insult to his majesty.

I risk that, too, when irony enters into my celebration:
this rebel claims the freedom owed, he feels, to his own dignity
and grants it to you and me, even while invading our space,
thrusting his torch of truth into our sensitive lives. He is
downright in demanding respect for his views – and even his vagaries,
born out of his oh-so-blithely spreading himself around,
and which his natural, open vanity even parades as virtues.

Women resemble art for pasha collectors – are a part
of their domain – adornment and supreme creature comfort.
With Shelley, he thinks love divided is not taken away,
but is he sure not to deprive any truer bond?
After the give and take of joy, he is inclined to scorn
the, to him, petty misery he leaves behind the scenes
when displaying to a new diva. And yet he's sorry later.
Ah well – if he truly believes he's allowed to play with fire,
then stirring starved flesh to pleasure sometimes is a way
of spirit – as Pygmalion woke and warmed his stone woman.

He fears the problems that arise when male prerogatives
are preyed on by a partner: tied up to another mind,
he'd fret at limited scope and possibilities pre-planned.
And security only stifles the straying undomestic animal.
But sometimes he develops a deep need of confirmation,
no longer to be a heartbreaker but to love right from the heart ...

He can be trusted, in Shaw's words, to play his game with a conscience,
to play and work hard, and his rampant optimism
pounces on the challenges to action and ambition.
Intelligence burns high, like a revived brand from the age
when evident reason sunned the naked form of man the measure,
when Enlightenment boldly rose out of medieval mystery,
evaporating grotesque fogs – and some hidden wisdom.
For Leo, standing as he does in the glare of his corona,
the problem is not to see the positive light, but to see dark,
with glimmerings of its own, which logic tends to overlook,
especially when it leaps into arrogant hyperbole.
Later, light relearns shadow and shapes a holistic view:
such as the world of lore that Jung ranged over, restored,
finding related shapes that speak the soul of all cultures,
mythologies emerging out of distance, out of depth.
He gave meaning to watery Memories, Dreams, and Reflections,
and ordered illuminated, life-informing archetypes –
like our signs, together making sense of the whole psyche!

Apollo is orbited by muses and microcosms of art
fomented by his brilliant care to come into their flowering,
corollas clothed in moving coloured language of the spectrum.
The sun-signed finds that fathering works is a natural function
of integrated sinews of thought, wish, will and act,
and circling eyes that recreate, enhance what they see.
Whatever beauty, whatever value, dilates his heart with vision,
he puts his arms around as if to feel the ideal as flesh.
Dear reality, if dull, is endowed with intenser pigments.

So imagine the figure of some great baroque artist:
like Rubens himself, no less, with leonine Ascendant,
he holds the centre stage, up in his enormous studio,

director of production of his paintings big as backdrops,
conducting his assistants with a flourish of his brush
and outdoing them all in his capacity for work.
A regulated chaos rolls out across canvas,
led by laws of dynamics along forceful courses – slowing
and stabilising to areas of clear, balanced colours:
full-bodied red – blue dreamy, breathing skyward –
yellow a dancing thought – and green lying quiet between them.
And gold! a fanfare in your face, or gleaming over the whole,
or overclouded but rimming from behind the dubious dark.
Even shiny extravagance or surface decoration
derive from that expansive rhythm of a wholesome pulse.
He fills world-scapes, wild or human: with cities, civilisations,
and always people, resplendent or pathetic or appealing,
serenely or avidly erotic – how he grips and wrestles
and strokes the curves of aligned limbs astride his solar wind,
stimulating stretched, compliant skin till it vibrates.
Can an artist of our time so celebrate life?

Prolific sun deploys among the poets his flares of fame:
Shelley, Hopkins and two Laureates at least – Hughes, Ted,
and Tennyson, Alfred Lord – his low, sonorous, gruff eloquence
glooms to a growl of doubt, but he records Victorian glories
and stoops to love a tiny 'flower in the crannied wall', wanting
to know God and Man. And such phenomena also gave
Hopkins, out of their selved inscapes, 'realer, rounder replies',
revealing God's grandeur. The vivid, muscled plastic language,
moulded to his will, bodily pulls the world together.
And through him its vigorous life is offered up in praise.
Leo has always longed to set muddled mankind to rights,
expanding from his centre to embrace us all. Mostly
avoiding the pose of the British lion: rapacious, patriarchal

imperialism, and on the other hand radical socialism,
he tried to enlarge and reform the old aims of liberal justice.
He also wanted, as artist, to wake the people's heart and mind.
Our painter's vast prismatic allegories partly parallel
the words Romantic writers so adored, even employed
as political philosophy: truth, beauty, virtue, love,
imagination – as if these form a pattern of primary facets
in Shelley's 'dome of many-coloured glass' filtering eternity.
Creative imagination is living fire for those ideals:
not only fluid fantasy, it captures, evaluates
truth – as the poet said, 'We must imagine what we know.'
That also means to see and cherish it all with a love
beyond passion. Over the whole broods the poetic spirit,
highest pleasure, which 'awakens, enlarges the mind itself'.
It revitalises good in an evil time and should reflect
corruption only in that light. That was the great hope
for artists as 'unacknowledged legislators of the world'.

The creative myth of the single soul is individuation –
learning to push its way out of moon mother's inertia,
clear of the omphalos bog and clinging umbilical serpent,
to liberate itself – to grow and know and tame itself,
for the sake of wider culture and collective consciousness,
the real gold of enlightenment beneath the showy glitter:
a far view of perfection Virgo will look into in detail!

Virgo (24 August – 23 September)

Now for a cool corner away from glare and blare.
Here, a quiet human animal, still tense
from too much of outside world, where belonging is hard,
draws her neat body back into its earth.
All-round alertness drops. Intent eyes
are turned down onto unstartling homely things:
habits, rituals, duties, various useful interests,
the present tense of every day, the day-plan.

I watch her select and fettle pens, pencils, paper
and microscope, and then arrange this and that
among a nature trove of shells laid on sand,
skeleton leaves, fractal fronds, pods, bones,
in grey and dun tones, with hints of jade or beige:
matter for morphology, founded and named by Goethe,
owner of great collections. – 'Now, teacher, explain!'

'It's one way the "world's innards are held together"
that fascinates the old Faustian nature philosopher.
Phylogenetic structures derive from basic forms,
all parts relate and evolve along with function,
ovum to imago, seed to flower. This thinker
also taught the psychology of scientific method –
dissecting, examining, docketing, ought not to distract
from felt experience of all life's interconnections –

we are involved in what we observe, even in physics.
I find it reassuring to fit into a pattern,
to know my own embryo echoed fish and frogs,
and a sense of wings hovers in radius, ulna, carpals.'

She's almost always active, but does not allow
study, work or worry to quite wear her out.
Once impeding problems have been thought though,
irritating particles removed from clear solutions,
like the pea removed from her princess' bed,
the fabric hemmed with fine stitches – when, that is,
she comes to a straight edge, the border required by order –
a break is earned. Maybe for early music, restrained,
as if evoked by Burne-Jones angels bending
pensive over plucked, struck or touched strings
(fraternal to her nerves?) – or Bruckner, spiritual,
or more astringent, twelve-tone works of Schoenberg,
who chastened to a system his post-romantic passion.

Or else we sit in the garden, among beans and berries,
asters and heather, admiring ants and worker bees,
with (elegant sufficiency!) a snack and a book:
perhaps a novel of tactful but intricate psychology,
perhaps verse, which could in fact be her own,
rhymed and regular, literal, often somewhat satirical,
wryly ordinary but touching – a bit like Betjeman.
A change is as good as a rest from scientific journals,
a verbal balm for busy brain and anxious heart.
And then a short walk. She notes along the path
stumble-stones, strewn bits of leaves and twigs,
a seed, a beetle on starry moss alongside –
the look and layout of things, as if she tries to learn

the language of nature's random, determined dispositions.
Small becomes huge: she dreams of Humboldt, how
he set his magnetometer in his garden pavilion
and then set about mapping up the whole cosmos.

Her reason is sweet to me, her uncommon sense
and level-headed perception of real inner and outer
particularity. And, as she explains to me,
'Method is so important, if not too obsessive:
drawer by drawer sorted, surfaces nice and tidy,
a place for every detail, every detail in place.'
But narrow inspection may neglect the bigger picture,
some leonine conception of a world of figures
of grand loose anatomy over coarse canvas:
I seem to see her peering through her lens, remarking,
she prefers the finish of Ingres – but it is worth restoring!
Her life's a terse design, where any crude line
ruins the whole, must be detected and deleted.
Quality control requires tight criteria:
validate the what, investigate the how –
the why? she drops her hands and looks into the sky –
and sees – not yet the answer, but her mutable Mercury
touching down to check what's doing at ground level.
His eye and hand, minded of harvest, mediate
minerals working upward, light working down,
from grain to grainy crown, the nurture of the crop –
cereals and other produce of close astute effort.
Nutrition does demand a decisive selectivity.
Each plant discriminates the useful from the harmful,
as does the bowel it ends in, with its endless job
of absorption, elimination, adapting out to in.
(Can we hear its plea that enough's as good as a feast?)

The principles of diet also include the cerebral,
suspecting the new, the non-rational even taboo,
till body and mind admit spirit into the trinity.

A fastidious digestion is doubled by the soul.
No wonder she has sympathy for small creatures
who register with round eyes or thin antennae
or whiskers and little noses the negative vibrations,
loud words, strident sights, contamination.
Many fears must be thought and fought down:
fear of shaky ground above eruptive emotions,
fear of the future, if not known then presumed,
and the risky road of duty, which her responsibility
has no intention to shirk. She sets up a routine
to guard against chaos, against oppressive muddle.
She checks, cautious cat, or circumvents eventualities.
'Be prepared! to stop things getting out of hand!'
It shrivels her, suspicion of people and of fate,
it makes her hang her shoulders, the corners of her mouth.
She snaps at me, 'If you don't want me to worry, then
let me make sure that things don't go wrong!'
I can't allay her alarms. As they are mostly rational,
I hope she's hard-headed and tough enough to cope.

She looks around to see where she can fit in.
To find her place means to present a low profile
and subtle coloration. 'I'm inoffensive, normal
and not an emotional poser manipulating you.'
This is only partly to avoid disapproval –
conscience does, indeed, make scrupulous cowards
and discretion is, she quotes, the better part of valour.
Projecting this image she is often undervalued

by those who mistake modesty for inferiority.
But when she feels respected, she can become prescriptive,
waving a finger at our offences: civilisation
means right conduct – first, self-correction
and then expecting others to behave themselves.

'This is what I'd tell them, if only they would listen:
turn the volume down and don't stamp about,
and don't make a mess in other peoples' lives.
Don't interrupt, be decent, keep your word,
tell the accurate truth – to keep the soul clean.
So, be good, sweet child, and if you can, be clever!
or at least be sensible and think what you're doing.'
Underneath the sharpness is a kind humour:
'Are you waiting for those dishes to wash themselves?
When they're done, I think we might put paid
to the day's account and then try to finish the crossword.'

She never told her love, its worked-out thoughts:
'He overlooks the low dull flower. I am,
for him, hardly exciting, but I'd feel debased,
ashamed of being garish, flirting scent – although
even *Mimosa* so-called *pudica,* sensitive plant,
is allowed its own aroma and its prickles, too.
I warn "don't touch!" when I think my upright reason
could be undermined, my pure mind polluted
(which does approve the worth of some immaculate goddess)
and, of course, when I assess the possible hurt.
Virginity's not the point – it is so annoying
when people can't distinguish prudery and morality.
And so I try to throw earth on my desire
and sandbag my heart against whelming feeling.

I do value solitude and can be celibate:
"myself it is enough". However, if he should come,
not to wash me away but to water my aridity,
like the plants I tend along with dead specimens,
the experiment of "elective affinity" might succeed.
Then I would be helpful but not interfering,
do my best not to repel with peevish bursts
of repressed exasperation, or edgy, clinical carping,
and not be too negative about his projects.
If I couldn't cure his faults, I'd stomach them,
waiting for a chance to forgive and be forgiven.
I would persist in love, as long as it was wanted,
and make my heart a place that's nice to come home to.
He could do worse than settle for that, I think.'

A partner's well and good, but one can be wedded
to work. She is in love with knowledge and is fulfilled
by scientific reverence for processes of life.
She was schooled to learn and to serve with all her skill:
and now researches into ways and means of medicine,
winding, precise-footed, neural, intestinal labyrinths,
charting the geography of personal microcosms.
Labouring in her rather culinary lab,
she knows how to raise the right response from substance.
Animal, mineral, vegetable are extracted, labelled,
reduced to their essence, potentiated, blended.
Fern root and fennel, cumin, calamite,
mallow, are her favourites and myriads of others,
edifying doses for the docile bowel-brain.
This modern wise woman finds the means to heal,
dedicated to life's down-to-earth magic,

linking quality, quantity and information,
and all correspondences in all variations
of significant colour and form, conferred by brown soil.

Agricultural issues cause her much concern.
Her other divinities, crop-carers – Ceres especially,
conscientiously reared and offered the corn ears
from plots cunningly slotted into the ecosystem.
Remembering that world, she groans, 'Look at it now –
greedy factory farms numb and poison the land,
like skin infested with parasitic monoculture,
or burnt, mined, built over – disastrous abuse
of matter by materialistic manufacture
divorced from need. The word "Economics" makes me sick,
degraded from the old sense of waste not, want not.
Growth – what on earth is meant by that? A kind
of cancer eating us up. We need food, shelter
and services, not wealth. But culture also depends
on exploitative technology – is it then naive
to long for a good poverty in a green peace?

'I was reading about Tolstoy. I value his work highly,
the detailed realism and moral earnestness.
He believed in the sanctity of work in the fields
and lived like a peasant, self-sufficient, simple.
He devoted himself to famine relief and wrote pamphlets
like "How much land does a man need?" and he founded
a school on his estate – a great educator.

'People in general ought to find the right teachers.
Confucius, for example (making a comeback in China),
had some good ideas, although too restrictive:

the noble individual develops social awareness
in regulated relations with family and others,
while preserving independent accountability.
That's the union of integration with integrity.
Mankind must know its limits (this is like Goethe),
apply its intelligence and recognise the risks
of blind activity – that's the union of reason and cosmos.
The human household wants a thorough spring-clean!
My poor hygienic soul is hyper-aware of insidious
physical, mental filth of mega- and nano-proportions,
hard to purge, expunge. Everything pernicious,
spurious and bogus, I'd like to see banned,
at least strictly controlled. Adverts are symptomatic:
perverting all that's holy. Try to understand
why I'm so finicky: it's because everything counts.'

Tiring, to cure with herbs and words the world's ills.
So she turns again to her inward dark mechanics:
not bemused or blinded by earlier moon and sun,
she takes the searching psychosomatic torch of Hermes
and glimmers like a hermit in her mind-cell.
Here, for instance, are echoes of a still-lurking
lion. Friendly and trusting to his wholeness, she means
to mould his force to mild strength under the law.
She knows the part he played in her continuing task,
the conceiving of the self – which might be her only child –
as if she nurses the seed of her own implicate order,
then bringing out a proven perfect life-loaf,
the daily bread. And so she finds her divine mystery.
I'll put my faith in that and let her get on with it.

Libra (24 September – 23 October)

We sit and look out over the lawn.
The temperate October azure waits
then drops to misty lilac dusk, behind
our barely substantial birches. It has been
a turbulent fulcrum of seasons, the equinox,
but now is a meditative time, between
fullness and letting fall, under the evening
planet. Swallows flicker around the skyline
and settle again – to stay? or to be gone?

I turn back to the room, back from nature
to civilisation, and contemplate again
the placid pastel decor – subdued elegance,
classical lines relenting sinuously,
favouring the disposition of books and paintings –
such as, facing our view, a Canaletto:
level musing light on an English façade
(discreetly ruled) in a half-formal park.
Below it, the table is laid ready for company:
fine-scented camellias in the centre
repeat the tone and careful curves of porcelain,
symmetrical among the glass and silver.
(Here, I imagine myself the wife of some
urbane Libran, linked with him partly
because of her own share of the airy Venus!)

What to wear? We help each other decide,
preening pair, approving of our feathers –
a muted flair, not frivolous, not severe:
his grey suit tones with my dove-mauve
plain satin (with opals or rose quartz?
and, on balance, which tie is preferred,
the pink or hazy blue? or paisley scarf,
amiable combination of both shades?).
This little trivial debate widens out:
are we overfond of appearance, amenity,
artifice parasitic on art, perhaps?
How real is the delight of the dilettante?
which does clothe deeper concerns now,
after the debonair, who-may-care,
liberating levity of our youth!
Now, my man is in his serious autumn.
Still, he dresses to match his nature – suave,
alluring and authentic. He refines
matter into grace of form and manner –
with smooth outline, just female enough,
sweet and vague, to alleviate virility –
and light and sensibility in his smile.

We live a pattern of complementary parts –
rational work and intervals of leisure:
the silent strategy of marital chess,
slow martial arts for equilibrium,
the consonance of a musical duet
(but duels demand too much heroic will!)
and concerts, exhibitions, invitations.

Libra (24 September – 23 October)

Our lifestyle is a model of its kind,
breathed over by the spirit of beauty,
so close, we feel, to the idea of justice.

Libra values Virgo's clever critiques.
His own mind, admiring, is inclined,
admittedly, to slide on fine surfaces,
but follows a loose-ranging measured logic.
And below the blue blushed-over sky
of his view, the grass seems less defiled, greener
than she thinks (but which side of the fence?).
He looks at both sides – pros and cons,
rights and wrongs or merely matters of preference.
He loves the pure conformity of equations
and settling down see-saws of paradox,
such as profane and sacred, precarious couple.
Balance is cosmic law. The pans must hang
free: Libra deliberates in liberty.
Then he ponders words for the weighed world,
like Eliot requiring the just sentence:
confident, but not ostentatious,
'The common word exact without vulgarity,
The formal word precise but not pedantic,
The complete consort dancing together.' So
dualities join in an all-round arrangement,
composite puzzle, where all aspects and complex
partial pictures adjust to make a whole.
The way from word to action can be wavery –
his indecision, uneasy, slightly nauseous,
weakens will and curbs spontaneous impulse,
but instinct for sanity firms the final move.

Feelings? this being hides in a thought-pagoda
from moody weather, outside or in,
from clouds, flashes, threat of electric wet.
Blustery, pouring emotion is bad form,
plunging and rearing up and down the scale,
the major–minor movements of a score.
Anger feels like hate, sick and guilty,
nerves are jostled by exorbitant joy
and warped concord feels like alienation.
If chords toss and twist, at least the staves
are required to remain even and notes in tune.
Hurt, held in, is not long resented,
the heart relaxes and head rises above it –
although he sighs quietly over the damage.

Our guests, anyway, find him well-tempered.
They seem to fall in with our Libran wavelength,
sounding a life compliant to the ensemble,
a moderated dialogue where discords,
stated with tact, tend to resolution.
We're all equal here, but my man's voice
is mildly cardinal in mediation.
Calmed under his reasonable beams,
we draw together and yet keep our place.
He is aware of others for themselves,
with wafting sympathy rather than watery empathy,
but still he discreetly tests his self-image,
comparing himself with them. He is concerned
he may be found wanting in the balance.
It is not weight, however, that's wanted here –
he undervalues the influence of his aura.

He brings up the question of sincerity:
'I often wonder if I'm too complaisant,
flitting between frankness and winning favour,
between Saturn and Venus, you might say –
Wilde's pairing of principle and profile.
And how about the importance of being earnest?'
We laugh. Then I think how good it is,
the atmosphere of agreement in this room.
Verbal fencing can be fun, but futile
wrangling, which is everywhere so rife,
only draws blood and bad feeling.
We come to the theme of culture and society.
Someone mentions the *Serenade to Music,*
now on the agenda for our choir,
first set, as our conductor tells us,
for sixteen singers – nocturnal conversation
like ours now. It ends on the word 'harmony',
in contrary motion of rocking, cyclic stillness,
like music of the spheres in 'immortal souls':
Shakespeare's and Vaughan Williams' mystic thoughts.
'And then,' I said, 'there is the famous quote:
"The man that hath no music in himself
Nor is not moved by concord of sweet sounds
Is fit for treasons, stratagems, and spoils"
no less!' But then my other half, disturbed,
judicial, 'That's too harsh a condemnation!'
Now a discussion: is culture in crisis?
sinking in the morass of the mass media –
has art lost its identity, its criteria?
Says one, 'If art can be anything, it is nothing,
some shabby object invested with a concept,
a fraction of the content of a book!

The message doesn't validate the medium
and the converse is the vacuity of design.'
So we wind around ideas of form
that flows in and out of core principles,
such as harmonic proportions, and grows great
on spirals of the golden mean symmetry.
This delights our painter: '– platonic love
of simple pure maths! like rose and lily
manifesting the souls of five and six –
and geometry of Islamic ornament,
form without content, which Wilde says
"reveals everything, because it expresses nothing",
suggesting a sacred beauty beyond form.'
But are we too afraid of its fragility?
Leo adores a perfection hidden in fire,
Virgo does try to clear the ground for it,
Libra conceives complete untroubled contours
in life as art, but dreads the fracturing
by Scorpio's essential confrontational content.

Loyal to what he loves, my man is moved
to give his creed: 'Good art is organic,
an energetic conscious microcosm,
also a meaningful, felt formulation
of deep awareness and thought beyond words.
It raises aesthetic emotion – the Indian "rasa" –
and may be a prayerful medium of the spirit.
Perfection? form prefigures but hardly owns it,
unless divinely empty, no longer human.
For the more-than-English composer, his holy temple
of sound hovers over an English horizon.'
Silence. We all reflect on an inner landscape.

And what about society and 'good taste'?
It should imply good food for the mind
and body – aesthetics should be wed to ethics,
where self-culture is also care for others.
Art for art, for people and for God.
In minds moved, self-moving, will to form
can purify will to power – and instinct, although
too much refinement enervates the heart ...
Eliot again: the liberal state comprises
education, civility, sensibility
and spirit. And, as in art and nature,
a working rule is unity in diversity:
various classless cultures (including elites),
like magnets, would attract and modify
but not suppress each other. What a dream.
We grope our way towards it – but too late?
Lost and gone? as even our group now breaks ...

Alone again, we two. I look at him
and remember the young peacock butterfly.
Single, he had a kind of lilting lightness
in ways of romance, like a Watteau gallant,
whose lute music is the food of love.
He blew hot and cold, bold and shy,
fickle, playing around – spoilt for choice
of girls so variously decorative!
But was it flirtation or friendship he was after?
Committed now to me, he does consider
my wishes or problems (often combined with his),
is self-effacing, even rather submissive,
but not blindly loyal – fairness is first.
In our duo, compatible parts run parallel

or counter – as when my separate momentum
stirs him to enjoyment or friendly joust
of strength – so we are matched in both meanings.

One plus one does not make one, although
two poles do constitute a magnet,
but if it splits, the pieces polarise
back on themselves again. A better image:
we build a bridge and meet halfway,
holding on to the swaying summit, trusting
it never will be broken through, baulked.
Or, crossing to and fro, we let go
the shore of ego, to stand by the partner
on his land. And last, the Libran emblem:
the scales (which also image opposite signs,
a Venus–Mars equinoctial axis),
the balance beam with arms in a coupled dance,
lifting, falling, pausing in counterpoise,
to rest at last around the stable centre.
Balance of temperament is given, but balance
of power, interests – accounts! involve direct
talk. And the symbol is also legal,
a primary one-to-one instance of justice
on its fine point. And there rests
the spirit of peace the law is there to serve.

So are we then the peace doves paired?
a bonding that once seemed to us the hub
of a huge wheeling movement. We remember
the anti-war vigils, vindicating
the power of passive resistance learned from Gandhi,
and sang with thousands 'give peace a chance':

our hope – for partners, friends, the state, the world,
for old free democracies now declining –
built on rule of law and right of protest,
working towards consensus, conciliation.

Hope still echoes ... but now, more and more,
the goddess will look to us for self-judgement.
Each soul must weigh itself, hoping
the last assay will find him feather-light,
ready for death. Meanwhile, this is for us
an interim before the death of the year –
and onset of Scorpio scorning an easy passage –
a middle-aged elegiac moment.

Scorpio (24 October – 22 November)

Now the fair balance is broken,
skewed skeleton under fog
jabbing at sky and at sod.
Our Libran's pleasant patio quakes,
a crude underworld exudes
excrementally onto his flower beds.

What did we do, any of us,
nailed onto the turning wheel,
to deserve all this? Must we be bent
to the worst for it to birth the best?
Put through it, put through it,
and some tempted to curse God.
I can't shirk this confrontation
with such raging saints, bedevilled,
waging their grim death in life
for holiness that costs them hell.
But! I do know scorpion-signed
balmy with a good sweetness
laid over their lacerations.
I think of them and take what comes:

A type – I face him here, afraid,
affronted by this Martian rebel,
his macho ethic squalid or Spartan,

Samurai-stark, karate-hard,
strict in black, white, blood-red.
Resistance, danger and drastic action –
he'll brave it out, take and give
strokes of destruction and creation,
compelling to his idea of completion
an end to which all means are good
(even potentials of petrol, plutonium?).

Onyx eyes, dark, sardonic,
hooded stare of bird of prey
or basilisk! drills into me –
out of the heavy iron and leather
helm of inscrutability.
Dare I refuse hypnotic hectoring,
when his scrutiny could accuse
a skulking worm somewhere in me?
Laser-sharp look and thought
bore to the mind's bone – intense,
he sniffs out occult causes
and gets to grips, to hurt – perhaps
to heal. And acerbic aphorisms
are curative, though dimly cryptic –
he wants me to face the facts of life.

Mythic places of his mind:
cave-temple, uterine,
with foetal idol holding a skull,
a horror and a hidden treasure.
Churchyard yews at Halloween,
aghast with ghouls. Night swamp
secreting slime-creatures, cold-

blooded, incommunicable:
but putrefaction is pullulating
precious life of threatened wetlands!
and high visions flying over.

Earth-water: and, universal,
the ocean bed of soul, unsunned.
He dives down in his cramped capsule
into the pull of sleep, the opiate
comatose pressure, where tentacle
taboos or submarine psychoses
grapple and uncase him – but then
a luminous world-formula looms:
the glow erupts, vital volcano
born below the miles of sea
that fixes and juts its jagged answer
against the sky, its molten passions
pour out of the heart and set
to fundamental absolute values,
all or nothing, good or bad,
casting in stone the soft humanity.

And then comes a quiescent crater,
a tarn – the surface ice-cold,
cloaking the catastrophes
of lava and steam from Pluto's realm.
There, Scorpio broods his furies
and his glories – extremes of feeling,
spasmic discharge in spite of cost –
depression or ecstasy, crawling, soaring.
Gods and grimacing demons bite,
the wound weeps, a mouth with teeth.

His own hand slashes his hand,
his self-scorn is a thorny whip
to exorcise the sins of the fathers.
Fear fascinates, shame compels
to rationalist oppressive order,
to puritan repression of prurience,
and sermons at the self-dug grave.

Two with Scorpio rising tried
to purge the age – Nietzsche, then Freud:
dredger of the dregs of mind,
detective or dissector of psyche,
to mend or murder the mad pain.
He slides down to your anal-genital
base of libido, eely instinct
lurking under crushing neurosis,
obsessive-compulsive, ritualistic
subjection to Eros and Thanatos.
He hunts hulking id, and ego
and superego stilted on guilt
and sublimation – subterfuge,
merely, of civilisation? not if
self out-knows the social constructs
and trusts the truth of poetry.

Here is highest and lowest – at worst
a villain coiled and virulent,
with lewd Rasputin's evil eye
and putrid predations, or inquisitor
twisting the knife, twisting your words
with traps and tricks, to extract from you
his own shadow – goading your guilt,

so he can control, he can condemn.
And at best concerned, committed,
generous, never forgetting a favour,
without envy and incorruptible:
impervious to outside opinion,
he will keep his own counsel.
If he must expose you, brutal,
hard on you, it's to test your metal
for some ultimate marathon.
His praise is deep-mined, precious,
his loyalty is unrelenting.
Refusing help, he risks his soul
to pull you out of a hellhole.

The old tale is done to death:
woman is hunted down, torn –
a rite to rob her secret of life.
Ambiguous Eve is eviscerated
or revered. Conversely, husky
Carmen trammels, castrates, sucks,
spider woman, the vital fluid.
Oh, the pulsing, revulsive urges,
eating, being eaten. The fall
through repeated fear and pain
into utmost orgasm of matter,
death-rebirth – the wet inside
of earth-mother for Oedipal sons.
Forbidden? is it sordid or sacred?
And, what is it snags together
sex, violence, muck and money?
the cack, the gore – the mucous scent
or stink of wealth, the oily power,

pollution and the dirty footprint?
(Yet, a Maecenas endows art
with abrupt magnificent donations:
Paganini, fiendish genius,
also eponymous to a casino).

This lover takes life by the horns
in flamenco insolence – inflaming,
baulking the black desire: bull
for the kill. In full pride of his piercing
look from under locked brows,
he offers himself, to be tossed down
into the fire of his own will.
His will – to find the one mate?
put on the rack to prove her faith.
His sarcastic mask hints at or hides
his need: possessive, jealous, vengeful,
in all his love-hate wars, the ideal
of the perfect bond, the double being
glimmers down his dark tunnels.

A Minotaur, man-bull,
is Picasso. His Ariadne, Anima,
should release him from his labyrinth.
But – her deficit of devotion
riles him, drives his virile volcanic
lust to revile, rip and mangle.
Salvation by love or art is denied.
His God died and the superman,
stifled in existential nothingness,
perverts his paralysing pity
for early blue and rose beings.

Scorpio (24 October – 22 November)

Seismograph of the subterranean
tremors of the time, he crucified
the blessing of his gift for beauty,
voiding himself in orgiastic
vomit of paint. Such works,
meant as weapons against nature,
are fetishes of natural magic ...

Niki de Saint Phalle is kin
to Picasso – and gobbles him up, too.
Her passions: 'scorpionic truth'
and God, and art her vampire lover.
Daddy and the patriarchy
she guns down in gobbets of bloody
paint – and then pities them.
Her snakes, vultures, death's heads
are grisly fun. The Nanas, gleeful
colour orgy and shape sorcery,
become birthing devouring mothers.
Her tour de force a Tarot garden!

How this sign does fight fathers.
Sylvia Plath, strong poet,
does away with the icon of Daddy
as some fascist bloodsucker.
Daddy – wrote her mate – fired her
like a bullet straight at God.
Her God is hurt by this world,
and over against the tenderness
for embryos in cold caves
under the vital visceral red,
death is a black-white perfection.

She practised suicide and succeeded
in '63, when Niki was still
at her ecstatic rifle range.

Picasso wrote one play,
on irredeemable evil. Director,
Camus, who connects himself
with Nietzsche – and with Dostoyevsky,
whose characters he calls fiery, icy:
in crime, punishment, virtue, depravity –
his inquisitor replaces God –
and can one become godlike or fully
human through even futile sacrifice?
And what of the free act of suicide
and what of debates with the devil?
(Think of Mephisto, Faust's shadow,
spawn of Goethe's Scorpio Ascendant,
or tempter of Luther's inky attack!)

Camus' Absurd is loss of meaning,
emptiness of slaughter and suffering.
'Nature denies us' – hence, revolt
of tense awareness and lonely will
in refusal of belief and hope.
Sisyphus is his apt figure:
chaining death, he angers Pluto,
its god, and like the world's workers
is punished with a pointless job.
And we are moved by the muddy cheek
and able hands against the rock,
pushed forever to the top
of endurance, forever rolling back.

But he is stronger than his rock,
taking on his fate, to make it
his tragedy of consciousness.
It can even be made good
if the rock is dedication,
authentic route from solitary
into solidary existence –
as in some desperate war on plague,
compassion for the still living,
wise care of the slowly dying.

In midst of life: a stuffed hole,
black dynamo bone box
caught in the crux of sex and death,
toiling through the thick of theology,
the tight maze of matter and spirit.
Bacon paints his screaming pope.
And Keats, who knew the stench of cut
corpses and world's giant agony,
said he found it wearisome
to 'question Heaven, Hell and Heart',
the vast broiling being of God.
And, doom in the bulb and light dying,
Welsh Dylan 'all-hollowed
man wept for his white apparel'.

Poor Scorpio – learn, no longer
to lash yourself for imperfection,
for not finding that final formula –
no longer grasp a fanatic narrow
blade to force heaven's door.
Turn violence to pure strength.

Full Circle

You have the grace of self-renewal
at some given time and place.
Great as visionaries are those
who dedicate themselves through love,
humble and truly high-flying.
Their sign is reborn a bright eagle.

Sagittarius (23 November – 22 December)

There! you flare at my mind: I see you flinging off the mire,
horse of spirit-fire! and climbing up to the clear plateau.
You stand and shake your forelock, to free your look over land,
over a haze and breeze of grass slanting away and over
old, broad woods and spreading conurbations and roads
that lead everywhere, under further finer lines of cloud.
Light, silence and all that empty space call you out
to cover distance and find a grand life horizon-wards.
Contemplation of endless otherwhere: and now, below
a coming storm, you feel a far view, lightning lurid.
A tremor trills along your haunches – arousal and release –
you rear and race, globe-galloper, laughing loud at thunder:
driving diagonal bolt or old Jove's bolt-bearer
Pegasus, pounding out the scansion, life-shaping rhythm,
carrying poetry to the unknown – or unicorn, also white,
with wide sapphire eyes and wise mind full of sky.

The father of gods, with chart in heaven, wields every weather,
the whole round, the whole play of coiling, colliding principles.
He opens his arms to nature, north, south, east and west,
like a kind of big engendering sun. In the guise
of smiling Ganesha, elephantine guru, Hindu Jupiter,
he's guardian of good tradition and guarantor of fortune,
and teaches that fullness, fulfilment kept in order keep us so.
You, arrow-man – you're mostly sporty, speedy, one-pointed,

restless distance-ranger – but that scope may be englobed,
at home in you, indulged in hefty corpulence, a great
sounding organ of total Miltonic (or Messiaenic) timbre.
Then you're like the large, loose, opulent and jolly
red-hearted planet, gonging terrific radio noise!
You like us, animals, humans, our anomalies and conformities,
magnanimous as you are, happy, expansive – with big A's –
or jovial's the word, with a big O – you enjoy openly
'Ohs' and 'Ahs' that answer the mighty fireworks of your mind,
complacent that honour is your due, even if we're reluctant
when you throw your weight around and take up too much room.
And temper? the tempest soon blows over, growling with remorse.
You live and let live (out of bounds if it must be?)
blinkered from evil – naive? blest? taking goodness on trust,
but fulminating against the false and harmful, where found:
insightful preserver of morals, morale motivator.
You put your hoof in it sometimes, into trouble, innocent beast!
with personal remarks or paraded, adored ideas, opinions
shouted in the resentful stupid street. However noisy,
yours is the sign of silence, meaning: not to blurt the spirit.
Milton feared 'presumptuously to have published' divine mysteries
and also Blake felt some reserve about his revelations.
But humour heals – ironic pathos homeopathic for pain,
or satire, pyrotechnic (as Berlioz said of friend Heine),
or mere amusement, with its mild muscle-relaxing power –
good vibrations: squeals and rumbles of serious contentment.
And benevolence buoys up, yet you often are made aware
it may be deflated by some sharp despair outside its sphere,
so you flop, flabby, your warm words peter out.
But, do keep the living breath free – stay with humanity!

Sagittarius (23 November – 22 December)

Always, your mind's in motion, rolling out across tracts
of voluminous erudition new and old, and broadens out
to hold and make it all your own – lived learning. You thrive
on humanities: philosophy, ethics, majestic metaphysics,
comparative religion glowing with ores of symbolic lore:
myths, fables, parables. It may be that random details
that litter the ground of here and now are overlooked as you lunge
towards future visions out there – part mirage?
as if your sight is hyperbolic – too far, too big, too general.
You don't see the single tangled trees for the whole wood.
But what a virtual university, synthesis of the universe,
massive magnetic head haloed by satellites of studies.
Holistic thought desires,aspires to, ever higher meaning
and asks: why? till wisdom swells and surges from the scalp:
your crown! like the cupola of some imagined monument,
the comprehensive space of an academy, library, archive
or temple. Its inner walls encircle a central panoramic
rotunda, a running documented rounding up of eras,
of ideas secular and sacred: arena that cups orchestral
echoed experience. Above, the domed, wide-angle tower
internalises a wind-rose of reality and revives
the outer world as imagination, in high lantern windows
in love with light. Made of a million slivers of crimson, gold,
purple, deep ultramarine, they recompose a pantheon,
pictures of all cults or of none – only of spirit.
(Today, an antenna thrills out its signals from the top,
shot as if by the tingling string of a noble bow at a venture.
And down in the dark a tiny dart traverses the world web.)

'In love with light', yes, and with the ensouling idea of love ...
But narrow, the nuptial gate you shy at, and the exclusive enclosure,
and worse, the stable. We bolt the door, but really ought to know
your spirit already bolted out beyond to your distant beloved,
impelled to master the hollow miles with outreaching resonance.
Absence lit by fantasy makes the heart grow, yes – but fonder?
diffuser? When conception outraces capacity, straying desires
might seem to compensate for feared falling short.
But freedom is a word of fire. And how it makes you angry
if integrity's mistrusted – as not always implying fidelity?
though jealousy can darken you, too. Where's a solution?

Before leaping to action, you take a round look, take in
the turbulence of terrestrial ages, climates and populations,
the social and personal fortunes of the swirling world. Which was
the ball his nurse gave to baby Zeus, to love and to play with.
He held it awhile in wholeness, in, through, above the trembling
but somehow self-determining chaos, which grows dynamic systems,
self-similar or varied forms on peripheries of patterns.
A Sagittarian still seems in safe hands, trusting
the unpredictable will be positive – that life will be
always supported by this free play of fixed laws,
through non-linear evolution: a big-wheeling lottery,
but one where he likes to hope that he, and we, are winners.
So he's a brave, slapdash rider through danger to opportunity,
nothing venture, nothing win – with eyes and mindset open.
When shifting enthusiasm settles, an overview is cast
of seas to span, land to map, developments to plan –
forces to deploy, to promote good corporate enterprise:
but power of growth promises now a devastating outcome,
and so you go on quests to save species – including humans –
and learn how to tackle global trade and cyber-networks

of organisations infiltrating like fungus. The total set-up
needs reworking, there must be renewal, not least of energy.
Is finance for it forthcoming over the gold-rooted rainbow?

Many fiery artists have a life-informing drive
to manifest their values, reveal the incorporeal, vastly
invest their love in highly complex, finely evolved constructions.
Far-sighted, blind Milton surveyed the world of his poem.
He covered, in the striding of his strong, lovely Latinate
lines and long similes all heavenly, earthly latitudes.
Inner illumination led him through his grand plan
for God, Satan, Man – his high-headed justification
of grim absolute deity: this debate is partly demonic,
doubtful, around divine foreknowledge and fate and our freedom.
Toiling out of a Scorpio hell, and chaos, and night, the poet
comes to holy light and looks with delight over his cosmos:
earth-centred, measureless but sphered in starry crystal
(yet, knowing Aquarian Galileo, he mentions another scenario!).
To regain lost paradise, Milton's Christ confronted Satan:
as did Blake's remodelled Milton – to redeem the devil!
Blake's marriage of heaven and hell is part of his prophetic
myth – all life is holy in his huge inclusive vision,
all religions are one, merging experience with wise
innocence in one search. This rhythmic poet-painter
of pleasure and pity, romantic priest of human imagination
and mystic mental warrior had his own – his well-known
'arrows of desire' – to initiate his flaming mission.

Now for music: I hear a concert created in that hall
inside the head. A symphony arches across colossal soulscapes:
fens, folded ranges, glooms, beams and stars. The blood
tingles under that radiation and thought seems to travel

the mind and body of nature. Sibelius, under Nordic sky,
waits, wide open to weather – out of soundless distance
comes a low hum and then remote drums, ominous,
then the strings' trepidation, tumult of dark gusts
that ruffle far, bleak lakes among Finnish forests.
Then a brightening – out of solemnity, strange exultation!
'Music can make silence itself speak' – that is its heart
of eloquence – Berlioz writes, in the fervour of his campaign
for true art. His own work aims at the 'great life':
among the crashing, whirling, are fine-linked, sinewy lines,
woven around a stilled space of transparent rarefaction.
And that's the core of the monumental, choral, quadraphonic
works (inspired by architecture of Milton's Pandemonium).
His language of timbre evolves its aural palette on a par
with coloured personalities of light. So the pervasive
but unfocused rays of passion are filtered by the prism
of artistic perception and send out their spectrum to the world.
Music stirs him as electric current along the nerves,
relayed out of the void with pure, irresistible verve.
And creation is a joy of will and discovery – like nature,
humanly felt and known in correspondences of moods,
dynamic motion, organic shapes, transformations of energy.
But children of 'flame-winged art' do fiery things coolly,
compelled by love to compel the work towards its own clarity.
They suffer in their love, when the world perverts, debases it.

He adores Beethoven – 'new world opening to our eyes',
into which his young, prancing soul is propelled, eager
to echo that Pastoral calm and storm in his own Fantastic solitude.
His words burn to explain that spirit. And words are all I have,
here, for music that transcends not only words, but itself.

The tone poet recomposes nature, as he wanders
through villages and fields, to works of 'more feeling than painting',
soundscapes of virtual being through keys of emotion and meaning.
The ground he walks marks the metre of basic tonic and dominant,
unless the bass shifts and groans in doubt of those fundaments,
and dredges down – till scales, arpeggios urged on spiky rhythms
rise on their parabolas like sky-searching rockets.
Elaborations of time expand to timeless variations:
the notes he wrestled with so long seem an improvisation,
newly pondered life that comes at last into a place
of meditation, a high space quiet with awed light.
There is the centre, the mystical idea, creative in chaos –
harmonic vibration through, beyond human instrumentation.
He was a man of bluff dynamics, electric ecstasy.
His hard way of wisdom takes us down through desolation
towards the glorious resolution to 'take fate by the throat'.
But then profounder, purer sadness grows into acceptance:
over the last quartet he writes 'must it be? it must be!'
and the notes dance away as if to a final 'that's that!'
His aim: to embrace the world with joy – and millions of us, he has.
Genuine being and inner beauty of art reveal a sense
of perfection behind creation, divined not devised – and truth
in spite of worldly ironies uncorrupted, luminous, healing.
Millennia may eliminate art – but let it last for us.

Now you – once the horror is sloughed off from hindered hooves –
take that thundering run of imagination out and away.
What land is open to your hope, what target legitimate?
Optimism curbed, aims matured, can always make
the best of things. Great structures need confirmed foundations,
inspired individual will can found laws – with help from Capricorn.
So hold your faith in fate, that good envisaged may be given
through world, space and all time – cyclic resounding epic.

Capricorn (23 December – 20 January)

An old tough goat man,
saturnine, would smile drily
at all the laborious notes I made
to condense him here: my awkward duty
to grasp his, and the silent soul
he won't show. I'll frame him fast
in four-square tetrameters,
dense – but have they enough dignity?
constructs of hard, heavy terms,
like the stones of the fort he holds,
his main office, centre of gravity.
Withdrawn behind a blocky desk
but dominant, he ministers,
priest of civic orthodoxy.
I apply to him – rather afraid
of severe texts extruded from
the bony face – until he grins!

The man is sober, controlled, sparse,
approves of salutary strictures.
Possessions: what's old, tried and tested,
manageable, of true value,
may mean security, status,
but otherwise are firmly renounced
as obstacles on the path of progress –
but care of money is merely reason.

What a long working life,
documented in angular dossiers,
nostalgic half-buried files,
antique annals, categorised
catalogues, systems conserving
genuine time-honoured survivals –
like the bona fide bones
of the inner man in an oak box.
And life is to be looked at squarely.
Concepts are reduced to essentials
in concentrated simple order.
Empiricism is almost compulsive:
the quarried thought his forehead fronts
forms a base of the real, solid –
a stable house – though fantasy might
wilt under the massive roof.

Repression of his private being
perhaps does prohibit his power.
And he may malinger – excuse
for not meeting his own standards:
he doubts himself, this ambitious,
superior, harsh, emphatic moralist.
He grouses 'that is not allowed!'
or cleverly he turns clown,
to play out his sincere judgements –
for Molière, humour means a mask
falling from the natural face,
as false falls from true reason.

Capricorn (23 December – 20 January)

The hypocrite who parodies goodness,
the world-hater's pride, the miser
who makes a tight fist of his mind,
in both senses betray themselves.

Negativity needs a retreat,
bear's cave where he bears out
depression, bitter deprivation.
Gloomy, leaden, wintry-stiff,
he fasts as if to forestall hunger
of separation, loss, denial.
His hide evolved from crab's carapace:
yes, he encloses a moist Cancerian
spot of yin in his yang limits!
Can emotional flow, confined
in a straight-sided reservoir,
be drawn upon for clarified use,
if acknowledged, but set aside?

Marriage: in time, he reckons he's earned
that institution so long revered.
Once a profound bond is achieved
(consistent with practical calculations),
he can be relied on to be honest,
dedicated and decisive,
supporter of the family ethos
and really kind, after all.
Love is so private, I wouldn't pry,
and words for it I'd rather leave
to his own blood-from-grit verse:

'I stand now on a rocky ledge
of life, edging to old age,
like a frosty fir whose bole
confronts the cold, high and sole.
As the slow planets wander
my pulse measures time – I ponder
outer bounds of brain and bone –
and I have learned to be alone.
But, love, we still have time
and my mind is still the same.
Say one word and I'll come down.
There is a house above the town,
to hold us safe in firm stone –
to be alone and not alone.'

Still, he reserves a reclusive den,
like a celibate, in the cellar
or attic – for ascetic hobbies,
important ones – schemes and models.
Work corroborates that self:
not tyrant or tycoon, I hope,
but self-made, his own norms
hewn from years of rugged struggle.
He sets out to remove mountains
(though some of them are only molehills).
Routine discipline, exacting
practice, tight coordination,
deep, aware, silent waiting,
bring at last ripe results.
What's worth doing is worth doing well –
from the ground-plan to the apex,
a strong, tectonic undertaking,

building the business – or body politic,
the social order of the State,
which respects and improves tradition.
Above all is the Rule of Law,
which Jupiter founds and Saturn enforces –
it's better to control than suppress,
better to assess than condemn.

Whatever his post, he won't desert it.
His own spine is a post, to support
the burden of office – image of Atlas
shouldering up the universe.
And here's a weighty matter for him:
astronomy. What a great array
of Capricornian, spaced-out
heads: Copernicus, Kepler (who
was also astrologer and proponent
of planet-music). And then Newton,
on his undeviating course.
In Kepler's wake, he worked out
mechanics of planetary motion
and universal gravitation.
Physics, too, invokes law –
as concept of force. And the *Principia?*
there maths moves supreme.
And optics? light-energy's palpable
properties imply immutable
particles of matter, in straight
lines and at distinct angles!
He refracts, that is: breaks, the hard
ray with the hard-faced prism.
Ah, the by and large demonstrable

beauty of science. What a wonder,
the way the solar family moves,
and mystery, how meaningful
it is to our lives down here.

But now we're shifted out of our system,
dimensionless and mind-blown
by superspace and supergravity,
by Hawking's exploding black holes,
space-time singularities,
the awesome two infinities coupled,
billions of tons compressed to a particle.
And all time looped in the lab ...

But back to our planets, splayed fruit
from solar root – back to Saturn,
who makes us take account of it all.
As artist, he chisels out thought
like wood or stone. Paint may seem
superficial – not to Cézanne.
Painfully, he mined nature
for permanent essential forms:
cones, fruity weight of spheres.
This pre-cubist is geological,
his intellectual structure sunk
in mass, bare of misty mirage.
Colour is split, prismatic, yet
somehow sombrely intense.
The ageing morose misanthrope
devoted himself to one mountain:
Sainte Victoire, with stark pines.

Arnold, poet of craggy profile,
is melancholy, forlorn, tender,
noble. From his critical summit,
echoing with lofty phrases,
he calls up authors in order of merit
and edits them, knocking away
any obstructive inferior stuff.
From classical models, his criteria:
plain impersonal objectivity,
moral and intellectual rigour,
sound subject and construction.
As Inspector of Schools, he required the State
to train the nation's best self.
Ideas of higher seriousness
were facts to be applied to life –
but to reach adored excellence,
'among rocks hardly accessible',
almost wears the heart out.

Says Tippett (writing on Cézanne):
we must forever reorder our lives,
our art, and force a new perception.
In *Moving into Aquarius,* he
orders his composer's reality
within the reality of his time.
Humanity, slow-formed like granite
by temporal forces, feels its spirit
inert, weighed down by wars,
technical materialism,
erosion of values by mass opinion.
Governments fear the persistent challenge
of socially dedicated artists,

who impel the collective psyche towards
the archetype of integration,
ritual marriage of light and dark.

He turns first on its dark side
the world of his oratorio – *A Child*
of Our Time – the scapegoat, put down
by politics. Tippett, himself imprisoned
for conscience, says it's up to us,
up to our moral compassion for all
the frozen in the labour camps,
the charred victims of genocide.
It is the capital value of art
to deal with this as well as rapture.
And even if Newton's laws are only
local – and all our wide, intimate
land a shrunk rock for Sputnik –
then 'what though the dream crack!
we shall remake it' over and over,
from 'rich impediments of Earth'.

Honour Capricorn, climbing beyond
the limits of ego and superego.
He won footholds one by one,
securing the steep track for others,
gaining, if need be on his knees,
a peak of aspiration – and sees
the sun winding up from solstice.
It lights a grave column that lifts
lore like lost fossils from vertical
time, bone cast in stone
and lessons lucid as quartz crystals,

essence out of pressured ages.
Engraved emblems formulate
fundaments of the shape of things
binding the future to the past,
illumination of ultimate truth.

Sidereal time, universal,
gives us our own moment, presets
planetary patterns. And Saturn
regulates manifestation
of what time endured brings:
through strict fate, a chance to learn
and pay debts. Through real life,
a way to healing rectification.

Aquarius (21 January – 18 February)

To mark the Age of Revolution, a revelation:
Uranus blew our minds really way out,
a quantum leap, to learn the beat of a new orbit –
and, for Aquarians, a long hop to and fro
from Saturn, old ruler of rules, to this reverser!
We also have to straddle astronomy and astrology,
sun-centred, earth-centred, both right.
No minds could have invented the mystical science –
truth found fixed on constellations, concepts
hung on hooks of stars! and every one of us
a woven ball of psyche, a fundamental tone
holding and unfolding its own full spectrum,
the planetary intervals of our development,
observing every god in turn round the amazing
cyclic mosaic of our charts. As for mine:
I think it's time to come clean and say – Hello!
I'm your writer, my sun is in this airy sign.
Still, the 'I' is re-imagined as the type ...

I helped to build Saturn's walls – they're worthy, but
my brain breathes in, more balloon than ball,
and wobbles over them, out to another air, somehow
somewhere else, as my awareness abstracts itself.
I sometimes take a thinking walk in a friendly wind
to discover – what? but do dislike damp and cold
that pinches poor blood and cramps weak calves.

How I admire my brave birth-time snowdrops: my frame
sometimes can't fulfil the scope of mind and will,
so I'm a mental migrant, ideas are my oxygen.
A Room of One's Own – thanks, Virginia Woolf:
I come back and sit alone at the high window,
my mind in clouds and nebulae, to receive, relay
to half-annulled earth, far bizarre signals.
But I also like to wave at people passing by.

I know who I am – or maybe it doesn't matter.
Odd bird, it hardly occurs to me to conform;
in fact, it's fun to baffle the bourgeois with far-out
original life-designs – that's my weird way
of being sane – with light self-determination.
Nose in the air, I don't see your slant glances.
Arrogant? Sorry. But do you know, my motto is
'I know' and I also know what is below my notice,
but don't mind admitting what I don't know!
Truth is many-sided, but nonetheless truth.
Dogma drags its feet while knowledge jumps forwards.
A freethinker, independent, planes over
science and para-science, and if he sees fit,
reorganises the lot, like another Bacon.
Synapses wire a widening labyrinth of data,
sparking across the gaps of a unifying theory,
a happy generalisation about the universe,
its holy infolded nodes of what, how and why.
Dualities, contradictions, paradoxes
once resolved, the circle stands fairly squared.
(I can do that, the diagram is in my notes.)

Aquarius (21 January – 18 February)

Reason reveals limits to reason. But intuition
glints behind analogy, wakes new awareness,
when separate spheres couple and take wing together –
wayward flight that lifts your whirring intellect with it.
Or drop your thought, throw some words up in the air:
alleviated, they flutter loose, aleatoric
(alea: dice – like ala: wing, freely fated),
then look how many lie in living rhymes of meaning!

Virginia might approve, but her profounder play,
blankly earnest, yearns for meaning – is it this?
is it that? Random items: a leaf, a wave,
a shadow, a laugh, a ball soaring, a hand raised –
make timeless moments that settle, steady things
into shape: art? life? art in life?
spirit flies to comprehend a whole world
in, beyond a London street, a blue bay.
The mind's tower is eyed with light, but one must leap
out from the top, freed by air, motion, vacancy,
and then, hovering hawk, swoop and drop on truth.

Nonsense invokes hidden sense or merely provokes
the overblown mind's membrane to deflate,
puffing out a laugh at sudden pointless jokes
or crazy caricature. The surreal is real satire
or just incongruous, like the dreams of candid Alice:
Carroll's chimaeras and conundrums test the child –
giving a civil answer, she's told: contrariwise!
She has to try to believe many impossible things,
like backwards living and logic – topsy-turvy world
of creatures on, or off, their heads, like the inventor

White Knight, the friend she always will remember,
a helpless, half-angelic, mild and shining figure.

Now, 'let's pretend' you're all invited up to my studio,
every singular one of you, or a casual group:
'Yes – come in, me dears, and take me as you find me,
informal, open, free. Right – mind the parrot –
now, look – surprise! quote: "it's my own invention",
a musical kite, with bells of light aluminium
tubes that look and sound silver, aerial dance
of intervals (or it could have electronic notes
made to react to wind movement – or, even more
ideal, a new hyper-aeolian harp's harmonics).
The bells are aural, the crystal structure visual, number.
I found this glassy fabric, more spectral than vanes
of dragonflies fine-tuned for aerodynamic
control. Tone and colour rows are poetry in physics,
pure language of sound and light curving upward.
Perhaps you have ideas? – Suspend a real crystal,
winking out the spectrum? – wrong size and angle.
Pity, beautiful thought. Anyway, when it's ready,
I hope to see it airborne, launched into the laws
of motion, risking the penalty of a fracturing flop.
Have we the right to flight? It should be a prayer-kite ...
art borne up by nature, radiant day-star,
or like a lark rising, its rare voice will fade ...'

I praise the work, not myself. Far be it
from me to make a false claim to afflatus of spirit.
What temptations: indulged ego, usurped height,
our lark-songs! and meant to bemuse, deter the merlin,
the claws of pain. Worse danger: if we fall

to the travesty, the flashy trap, the low lure
of a lark-mirror, mirage of sky to bring us down.

Honour near-perfection of art near to tears.
Here are three Aquarians: Mozart, Schubert, Mendelssohn.
All of them died early and have an ageless air
of innocence and clarity, a serious lightness
over, above shuddering horror and utter sadness.
The same year Uranus appeared, Mozart
burst from palatial patronage to become freelance.
His operas come close to people, nobles and commoners –
the sober and comic, the spiritual and the natural man.
The quest of philanthropy, friendship, inner growth and faith
is led by the magic flute towards the sacred love,
marriage of sun and moon, image of integration.
He went alone to his grave in the snow. And I have heard
that only evolved ears can take his light in death.

Schubert's melody, long, endearing, is offered to friends,
yet he muses on love, loneliness, like a stranger
always leaving, until the winter wandering ends ...
My words flag. Oh, would he mind a mild joke?
Perhaps I'm flippant, pushing away the frozen pall –
but must mention – he wrote *The Looking-glass Knight!*

I love my friends. Our lone minds link and waft
a warm current between us. What's a good word
to correspond to 'friendship'? I know – 'correspondence',
separateness and sharing, preferably *my* interests! –
fantasy-fiction, computers, art, aviation,
horoscopes, humour, sport – the uplifting sort –
as long as my legs allow, I will sprint and spring

and flick the fledged shuttlecock to flirt with gravity,
like the thoughts that glide from me to you and back.
Authentic thoughts and words – if not I challenge them
or only stare in silence, with a raised eyebrow.
I'm frank, opinionated, I think I'm fair-minded,
I have no real malice – and I do want to be helpful.

But how do I relate to humanity as a whole?
Oh, how it makes me wince and weep in my soul,
the nastiness tangled up with fear. Ah – look
how great writers show but grow above grimness –
Dickens amuses, moves me, I soften towards his poor
vulgar, plucky, poignant, funny, eccentric people
and those persistently good in muddled hard times.
And oh what larks we have, what affectionate laughter!

Of course, with life predigested on the page,
it's easy to empathise ... I do enjoy company,
yet sometimes feel alien, cold, on another plane,
tempted to scoff, with Alice, 'You're just a pack of cards!'
Futile dispute gets on my nerves and tedious talk
bores me – then I become rather remote – drifting
off to the window, I'm atomised into the blue ...

Passion? well ... the earthy body used to be
beneath my view. I sought only the inner seraph
of self and other. I floated up above the drag
of emotion, in a thrilled thermal of heady ideals,
like an ethereal androgyne. The dream of art
was love that would not lame, but elevate, empower.
I soared into that sun – my fraying wings fanned
the fire – it beat through me, rosy Icarus – then,

burned, deplumed, my freedom was a catastrophe curve
down to wet and visceral mud – a foundered gull
gaping and blinking. So, not such a bright idea,
was it. But are we wrenched from spirit to be led back?
Breathe deep and let the cloudy turbulence
of delusions calm and clarify to real feeling.
Hope to offer up whatever you have of wisdom,
for a cherished partner or else for some friend,
on his own road but always in hailing distance.

I am in love with take-off, lift off, levitation,
looking for release – and research. Following Capricorn's
lead upwards, it's up and away off his peak,
treading air, to land – we hardly know where.
We fly with Lindbergh, or Piccard balloon-blower,
who inflated his ambition into the stratosphere,
chasing cosmic rays from space. Now face facts:
proud pioneer toys are purloined for war.
And now we're truly up and out of solar bounds,
with *Star Trek's* Picard in his mission for peace,
a universal federation backed by weapons.
Superhuman hubris ratiocinerates
our ends, ever since that fond Prometheus stole
forbidden fire to promote our progress, our enslavement
to man-made detritus, debasing brain and body.
What was never made needn't be recycled!
Refuse, especially atomic, is with us forever.
What heroic Hercules could now muck out
the squalid stables with an unequivocal river
of mind from a modern type of Aquarian urn?
And art's not exempt from taint: what does it cost
the earth, all the equipment for music, painting, books,
and what industry isolates my aluminium?

A closed society throttles knowledge: ruling clerics
feared their tower of authority would be stared out
by Galileo's high point of observation.
Astrologer, too – but proved the sun stays, the earth
moves – then had to recant, a crime against the truth.
Yet those fears were not unfounded. Bert Brecht
pins the dilemma under the lens of his play and sees
as Promethean progeny through this Father of Physics and through
the Father of Experiment, Bacon – the ultimate Bomb.
But how sad that the ivory tower of science is suspect.
It seems we can't shove genius back in his bottle
or drag with bitter epic effort the One Ring
of Power to be unmade in the fire where it was forged.

We try and try. That is a grand tale of Tolkien,
blending Capricornian sun and Aquarian soul:
speak 'friend' and enter the lovely myth of truth,
early earth a heaven, made by breath of music
echoed in language of elves who move under stars,
till many lands fall to filthy widening waste.
A fellowship is formed against the foul shadow
and good even fights temptation of power for good.
Only a modest Hobbit can bear out the quest,
strengthened by acceptance of sorrow, pity, sacrifice.
And then, a lull. But many are leaving Middle-earth ...

Where on earth was, or could be, the Golden Age?
Utopia? More's great pun of noplace goodplace –
a State open to reason, virtue, higher learning –
and free belief, though all worship God together.

Aquarius (21 January – 18 February)

A commonwealth with no money, no greed,
where all work and only take what they need.
Insular order – but ours is one snarled-up world.
In my youth, ruthless and simplistic, I wrote
on one page a plan to put it all straight:
cut overproduction and the profit motive,
curb at least the creeping stress of computer as virus,
ban occupations which involve harm
(that's most of them). Result: massive unemployment.
And so the core problem is overpopulation.
Now, these big statements breed endless issues:
enforced birth control? Galtonian eugenics?
Not allowed. So what's to be done about that girl,
disabled, with a baby she can't bear to give up?

Yet some utopian hope of reform always grows
on vague but good principles of revolution:
responsible freedom. Fraternity or rather friendship,
multicultural. Qualified equalities
of opportunity and treatment, not of values –
they must not be stifled by a stupid majority.
And education, for the life of the whole person.

The story of earth is evolution, more or less
as Darwin told. It bred the New Age of Aquarius,
electronic, esoteric, on course to explore
and verify knowledge: inklings, insight, clear-sight,
the nous of neuroscience, the acausal and causal.
We find forms working throughout coloured chaos,
until broken musical measure, deranged spectra
ray out in new ways through matter and mind
(conveyed now, if not corrupted, by cyberspheres).

Full Circle

My sign, like others, has a small elite of light,
above my own overwrought ideas, that hubris
that hides in self-mocking humour – ironical, distant –
and must be humbled, move closer in to commitment.
Wise ones know that with our thoughts we make the world,
that terrible things can easily be done on principle,
that 'light-bringer' can be translated as 'Lucifer'.
But selfless in self-knowledge, masters become servants,
giving up rebellion to find inner freedom,
pouring science and spirit from Uranian urns.
Illumination is cold, until we're able to care,
having glimpsed heaven, for reality down here.
If we fly up, we should bring down light –
and warmth, also found in the upper atmosphere.
To live out that love, we're led to the last sign.

Pisces (19 February – 20 March)

Now, for the last time, I'm drawn down to encounter sea.
I stand unstable on the sand, my feet sink, I stare
and doubt the shape of things and my horizon that centred me.
My mind, unmoored, is drifting out in sliding haze, to find –
under sleek skin and sibilant seethe of the dizzy flow –
Neptune's light and dark double fish that shimmers up
and shrinks down, its own shadow, into the unconscious.
Seas, rivers, clouds are a cycle – perspective always shifts:
now back to the pool, where years ago I peered down
to birth a symbol for the myth I sighed after: Psyche!
evolving soul's epitome and avatar of art.
I tried to take up tenderly, palpate the vaporous fable,
vacant inexpressible wraith, wisp of water's breath,
surface-haunting water-fly, dim former nymph.
It was my old dream, my poem from under gleam and foam.
Fading fairy ... in awe of your aura, if I dare to grasp you,
I'm left with merely a smear of dismal powder on my palm.
Oh, I know, shape-changer, how you muddle my metaphors:
fish, fly, phantasm – even as female human, you form
a simulacrum still vague, veiled in watered silk,
in ectoplasmic layers and folds, a sheen of algae-green –
or, portrait of a normal girl, there yet not there ...
A painter brings us nearer to the feel of her, her ambience.
He softly irradiates, Renoir, the bemused moment, the mood,
among wavering lines of reflections, under mottled shadows,

all a blur of coloured atmosphere. The light of a day
of leisure seems to stroke the sweet sloth of boaters, bathers,
and gloss their dingy lives. He seems to brush a discreet love
over blooming skin and luminous hair – contours blend,
not divide, the interflowing beings, leaning together.
My Piscean has a tenuous touch on life, hoping to slip
loosely through, slowly. There, she sits and droops a dimpled
sleepy face on a small hand. Her words, when they come,
are fluvial music, until her fingers creep round to mute them:
she does and doesn't want her sense to seep through. Silenced,
remote semi-spectre that lost the energy for sonority,
she only smiles with upward eyes – a last ancient light
over a private island: it wafts oriental perfume
like the pure phrase, unheard but warbling down the memory,
violin voice of Scheherazade, leading from story to story
over heave of sea that sailor Rimsky-Korsakov sounded.

The vast passive swell of mind also implies minuteness,
as in intimate streams, wherever frail osmotic fibres
of lazy lank weed are dimly moved by occult currents
under minimal ripples. Out of this home of larval hints,
a rare imago emerges (in fact, just now! I was reading
the defined name in flitting italics: *Hydropsyche instabilis,*
a smudge of wings in watery dusk, with ultra-fine feelers).
And other obscure organisms are fringed with sensitive cilia
to filter faint codes – and even, embedded in our heads,
filaments in the cochlea, secret well, sieve the tones
that fuse to music – modulation of universal motion,
all that surfaces and sinks, uncannily convected.
What a test, to net in verse this Piscean perception,
dispersed swarm of viscous, invisible animalcules or massed
bubbles in shuddering lumps of spume. And yet this mentality,

coursing from source to ocean, can view all-infusing systems,
principles polymorphous but single – synthesis from analysis.
This psychic sleuth of holistic truth completes detective Virgo.
So musical Einstein interrelates a universe of movement.

The unconscious is cacophonous chaos. But winding from below
are amazing fugal loops that make meaning. The hidden ear
delicately picks out the parts, in correspondence,
like sundered particles in tune over time and space.
Chains of symbols trail below the trance of closed eyes.
And upwards, vestigial eye, the pineal window opens out
onto the paranormal, lapping its waves over the world,
an awareness that consoles or overwhelms. Hence, temptation
of drugs to muffle suffering sense or to induce visions:
but then elusive, true mystery turns to mystification.
Delusion always dances with divination, with belief.

A negative Neptune child belongs nowhere, treads tentative
or curls up unhardened feet in some flimsy retreat,
at home only in the hidden, behind sliding doors
of fantasy. When life, lewd and loud, tortures her,
she thins it to a flickering film or holographic phantom,
or watery sphere with oily illusory colour-veil that swirls
the spectrum some have strained heart and brain to hold straight –
but so it englobes free beauty of true imagination.
When sensibilities are soothed, the mind can see whole,
in oneness with the all-in-all, belonging – everywhere.

Shoals of feeling veer, driven: only think how soon,
in this tremor, silver rainbow-touched membranes tear.
How vulnerable, the heart of aristocratic aesthetic reserve:
never let your face show your hurt, said Chopin. Yet,

this piano-poet moves from subdued musing to passionate force.
Sad, fastidious exile, he shunned the wide public, but dazzled
the salons, then sat pale, ailing in cold Valldemossa.
The hands mastered the slight body's turbulent mortality
and sounded out the noble glimmer under intimate woe.
In wordless tales and hypnotic circling of disembodied dances,
figured light sprays up and plunges down, torrential,
and lingers on in pools that lie reflecting the unearthly.

The heart-swell of wishes for the futile or impossible
or wrongful or even for one's own and the greater good,
subsides again to avoid unwilful damage or disappointment.
What the phobic Sibyl desires or dreads is not apparent,
feeding on the dark flooded underside of mind.
One dread: of becoming a crazed, effaced ghost that craves
oblivion, easier option than the revered real nirvana,
end of the unending, imperceptible path of enlightenment.
And how much safer it feels to be invisible and nameless,
an underplayed person, unwilling to put oneself forward
or to take advantage. To be feeble or proud of subtle strength
and wary of it: the various levels are closely overlaid.
Almost as if ashamed of lurking shades, the flesh starts
at sharp satire, and shivers away from any supposed hook.
It's natural, too, to adapt slyly to an expected image,
then slink away from demands, to avoid having to say no.
A moral stem that ought to stand upright under pressure
tends to twist in half lies and cowardly denials.
Plausible paradox: this flexion means to maintain fragile
integrity of free growth – so what's the worth of truth?
until one learns that subterfuge does fail trusting love.

Pisces (19 February – 20 March)

Positive and negative are peaks and troughs of waves,
are ebb and flow. Her tides of sympathy always return, with time
to listen to your life, even without words. And pity
for world pain floods over and over, as if it could
dissolve it all along with all the poison of corporate guilt.
This susceptibility leaves the system open to gloom,
likely to spread to others unless her good magic grows
and lives to heal and save bodies and souls (Neptune symbol:
a legendary dolphin-spirit that lifts us up from drowning).

Marine Venus, elevated here, is mirrored in multiple
phyla of water nymphs and sirens. No need to name them,
by their names you can't know them, these subliminal larvae
of man's Anima. Do they lure only with fey reserve?
but if they loose their clinging hair and wind their incantations,
cover your eyes and ears, and don't pursue when they turn tail –
or do! and before they pull you under, hold and haul them home:
those not yet quite human will be crying for a soul.
Peripheral, these. A real Piscean woman is full-ensouled
already, with dreams of union as diffusion in the universe –
only despair, delusion can make her selfishly sentimental.
Once she comes to rest with someone, the stream of things is quiet,
though muddled by querulous cross-currents in silted-up meanders.
But if you're drawn on to crash through, or impose direction,
you only inculpate yourself. But how could you follow
the murmured sub-song of furtive hints? Your exasperation
is mutely taken to heart, until distress bursts out.
She needs emotional mutual care, in long-forbearing peace.
So handle subtly her fear to offend, her unobtrusive love,
and wake the cocooned radiant core of this potential angel.

The spirit of ideal work is strong, bodily will is weak:
the spine sags, hands and feet shrink away from earth,
retreat into the surf that unravels, rocks urges asleep
or flattens them out, backsliding over sand. Liquidity,
however, won't be compressed by strictures of rigid intellect,
but is a way of faith in old infolded natural order –
'confusion', after all, can mean productive 'pouring together'
and even evasive debility makes a space to learn and create.
And old ruler Jupiter opens up to possibilities
of wealth, success, eased along by dignified indifference:
if nothing really matters, it seems everything can be risked.
Salmon, after all, smooth muscle against the slope,
taut with purpose, fling themselves up into their own.

Wonderful things are done by the loving altruistic anonymous.
They give themselves to body-mind-spirits maddened by misery
or dire addictions that drown in fake ecstatic, expansive calm.
Supposed release from matter only brings enslavement to it,
narcotic compensation for pain concocts a worse nightmare.
Wounded healers know the threat to psyche and cells – and know
the viral vice of negativity, swamped in hypochondria.
With laying on of mind's hands, prayer, prana, harmony,
they put life in balance. Thousands work in a holy name,
like the name of the man, emblem a fish, who once revived
lame legs and blind eyes, and gave his hand to raise
Jairus' girl, who lay dying, and Lazarus out of death.

Therapy, not only cathartic, is one gift of art,
through its independent life. And artists need strength
and form or they may become discontented failures –
and anyway, ambition for personal fame and self-expression

is not very Piscean. But, what brilliant exceptions,
with enchanting sensitivity and other-worldly finesse,
though self-communing can be almost beyond communication.
Devoted Mallarmé was desperate to rhyme his ineffable theme.
His Faun's fantastic pipes of primeval breath do sublimate
at least the indolent afternoon, the lost whiteness of naiads,
but that intoxication also obliterates his ideal,
naked behind the musical drowse. Unnamed, or only 'Azure',
this is abstract, pure, not as a maths curve is conceived:
but only a negative, flower 'absent from all bouquets', or silent
sound that haunts a vacant sterile shell, or emanates
from void mandola or hollow viol of ancient saintly icon.
Impossible art out of nothing? the mere attempt torments him.
Languid, alone, his impotence is a long yawn, a fog
to hide him from his god. But his phrased awe is potent,
the numen of his non-existent rose evoked from dark.
Verbal music: and it was voiced out by Ravel,
secluded in precious rituals of perfection. His language
of artifice and nature, partly learned from Chopin, conjures
refined impressions of delicate scenes, in sensuous ambiguity
of unresolved harmonies. He notates the light of water,
mirror-still or thrilling up, a million distinct drops.
Stirred, he needs to sway himself to sleep in a cradling boat ...
And there are nymphs, too, animal fables and childlike magic.
The pleasant pliant surface-play overlays the pathos,
the pity of innocence. Then a ghostliness gathers, grows loud,
grotesque, while he waltzes his era of war to a frenzied end.
There's water-music for animals, and the wise child in the adult,
in Kenneth Grahame's river world: Rat, and nosing Mole
far from home, laze about in boats under the willows.
Later, they're floated into a kindly vision of Pan himself,

divine piper islanded in the stream. The dawning notes
lift them up on a mystic wave and turn their limbs to water.
The fading of that is frightful loss. To be happy, they must forget.

The Ram began: here I come! the Fish, ready to finish,
whispers: I'm going, going – more than ever world-weary
in our deranged time, that grips the brain, gripes the gut.
Is Arthur Dent an Everyman, galactic hitch-hiker
of Douglas Adams? homeless, lost in the horror, lost for words.
But there is still tea, and lying around in addictive sea,
porous to the polyphony of it, and messages from its fauna,
departing dolphins – as if man has an aquatic past.
And Adams counters nihilism with wonder at the mystery
of art that can encapsulate cosmic mind as artist,
the growing infinite glory of fractal patterns, winding webs
of world-as-maths-as-music, resolved as one tune: by Bach!

He, 'Brook', is oceanic. Although his primal dynamo,
the happy mechanics are Aries, his Neptune is in Pisces,
with Mercury and Venus. So he links first to last.
All his music is worship and becomes what it worships.
And timeless lyricism, elegiac or warmly affirmative,
rolls life through all levels and lights, until we feel
ourselves distilled as drops in mist, each holding the whole,
endless aura of inconceivable colour and sound vibrations.
And if all this darkens, falls away, he consoles, redeems,
singing us into the end of suffering, into good rest.

If we practise dying we practise freedom, say the wise.
And a way of being rootless, empty, alone, can end fear,
expectation, illusion, even desire and despair of perfection –
a chance at least of innocence and unenforced virtue.

Pisces (19 February – 20 March)

Inclusive care, compassion for pain, become natural action,
undemonstrative, not creating obligation or guilt.
So the spirit can let go of ego, can grow and permeate
the existential vacuum sealed into our solid world.
At last comes a silence beyond the archer's humming string,
beyond the mountain's raptness or inaudible words of space.
There is love of spirit which is beyond imagination.